MASTERING HEAT TRANSFER: 5 GTU SOLVED PAPERS

(FROM CONFUSION TO CLARITY: PREPARE, PRACTICE, AND PASS YOUR EXAM)

First Edition 2025

PROF. ALPESH V. MEHTA

Mechanical Engineering Department,
L D College of Engineering,
Ahmedabad.

NOTION PRESS, INC.
800, WEST EI CAMINO REAL #180,
CALIFORNIA USA 94040

DEDICATED TO

STUDENTS.

PREFACE

In the journey of engineering education, **Heat Transfer** stands out as a crucial subject, forming the foundation for many advanced concepts in thermal and mechanical engineering. However, for many students, especially those preparing for **Gujarat Technological University (GTU)** exams, this subject often poses a significant challenge.

To bridge the gap between classroom learning and exam success, I am pleased to present **"Mastering Heat Transfer: 5 GTU Solved Papers."** This book is designed with one clear goal: **to help students confidently prepare for their GTU examinations** by providing fully solved past question papers in a clear, step-by-step format.

The solutions included in this book cover five recent GTU Heat Transfer papers, each solved with detailed explanations, relevant formulas, and proper application of theory. These solutions are aligned with GTU's examination patterns and are meant to help students:

- Understand problem-solving techniques,

- Clarify fundamental concepts,

- Practice efficiently, and

- Build confidence before the exam.

This book is not just a solution manual—it's a tool to **master** the subject through real exam practice and conceptual reinforcement.

I sincerely hope that this book proves to be a valuable resource in your preparation, helping you achieve both academic success and a deeper understanding of Heat Transfer.

Thank you for choosing this book. I wish you all the best in your exams and your engineering journey ahead.

JULY 2025   **ALPESH V MEHTA**

Acknowledgement

The successful completion of this book, *"Mastering Heat Transfer: 5 GTU Solved Papers"*, would not have been possible without the support, guidance, and contributions of several individuals and resources.

First and foremost, I express my sincere gratitude to **Prof. A.V. Mehta and Prof. P.G. Choksi**, whose book on **Heat Transfer** has been an invaluable reference throughout the development of this book. Their work provided clear theoretical foundations and practical insights that greatly enriched the quality and accuracy of the solutions presented here.

I would also like to acknowledge the evolving role of various Artificial Intelligence tools which were instrumental in assisting with content structuring, formatting, and clarity enhancement during the compilation of this book. These tools served as effective aids in refining explanations and ensuring consistency, all while upholding academic integrity.

Special thanks go to my mentors, colleagues, and well-wishers who provided constant encouragement and feedback during the development process. Lastly, I am grateful to the students of Gujarat Technological University (GTU)—your academic needs and challenges were the true motivation behind this work.

I hope this book serves as a helpful guide in your exam preparation and strengthens your understanding of Heat Transfer.

Contents

PAPER 1_ 3151909: HEAT TRANSFER

SUMMER 2025 EXAM   DATE: 15/05/2025

Q.1 A) Define steady-state heat conduction. How does it differ from transient heat conduction?

Steady-state heat conduction is a condition where the temperature at every point in a material does not change with time. This means that although heat is flowing through the material, the amount of heat entering and leaving any part of the material remains constant over time. As a result, the temperature distribution remains the same.

The main difference lies in how temperature changes with time:

- In steady-state conduction, the temperature at a given point does not change with time.
- In transient conduction, the temperature does change with time until it eventually reaches steady-state conditions.

B   Explain Fourier's law of heat conduction. How does the temperature dependency of thermal conductivity vary for gases compared to solids?

The French scientist J.B.J. Fourier who proposed the law in 1822. It is an emperical law based on observation. It states:

"The rate of flow of heat through a simple homogeneous solid is directly proportional to the area of the section at right angle to the direction of heat flow, and to change of temperature with respect to the length of the path of the heat flow."

Mathematically, it can be represented by the equation :

$$Q \propto A \cdot \frac{dt}{dx}$$

where,

Q = rate of heat transfer per unit time; W

$Q/A = q$ = heat flux ; $\dfrac{W}{m^2}$

q = rate of heat transfer per unit area per unit time; $\dfrac{W}{m^2}$

A = heat transfer area (normal/perpendicular to the direction of heat flow); m^2

$\dfrac{dt}{dx}$ = temperature gradient; $°C/m$

dt = temperature difference on both the side of walls; $°C$

dx = thickness of body in the direction of heat flow; m

Thus, $Q = -K \cdot A \cdot \dfrac{dt}{dx}$ ...(1)

Temperature Dependency of Thermal Conductivity:

- In Gases: Thermal conductivity increases with temperature. This is because, at higher temperatures, gas molecules move faster and transfer more energy during collisions.
- In Solids: Thermal conductivity usually decreases with increasing temperature. In solids, heat is mainly transferred by vibrations of atoms (phonons). At higher temperatures, more

atomic vibrations cause more scattering, which reduces the flow of heat.

C **With usual notations derive general heat conduction equation in Cartesian coordinates and explain its significance.**

For the thermal analysis of the bodies having shapes such as walls, slabs cartesian coordinates are used. Consider an infinitesimal rectangular wall of sides dx, dy and dz parallel to the three axes (x, y, z) of anisotropic material.

Energy balance / equation for elemental volume is obtained from the first law of thermodynamics as:

$$\begin{Bmatrix} \text{net heat accumulation} \\ \text{from all the directions} \\ \text{in the element} \\ \text{(A)} \end{Bmatrix} + \begin{Bmatrix} \text{internal heat} \\ \text{generated} \\ \text{in the element} \\ \text{(B)} \end{Bmatrix} = \begin{Bmatrix} \text{Heat stored} \\ \text{in the} \\ \text{element} \\ \text{(C)} \end{Bmatrix} \qquad ...(5)$$

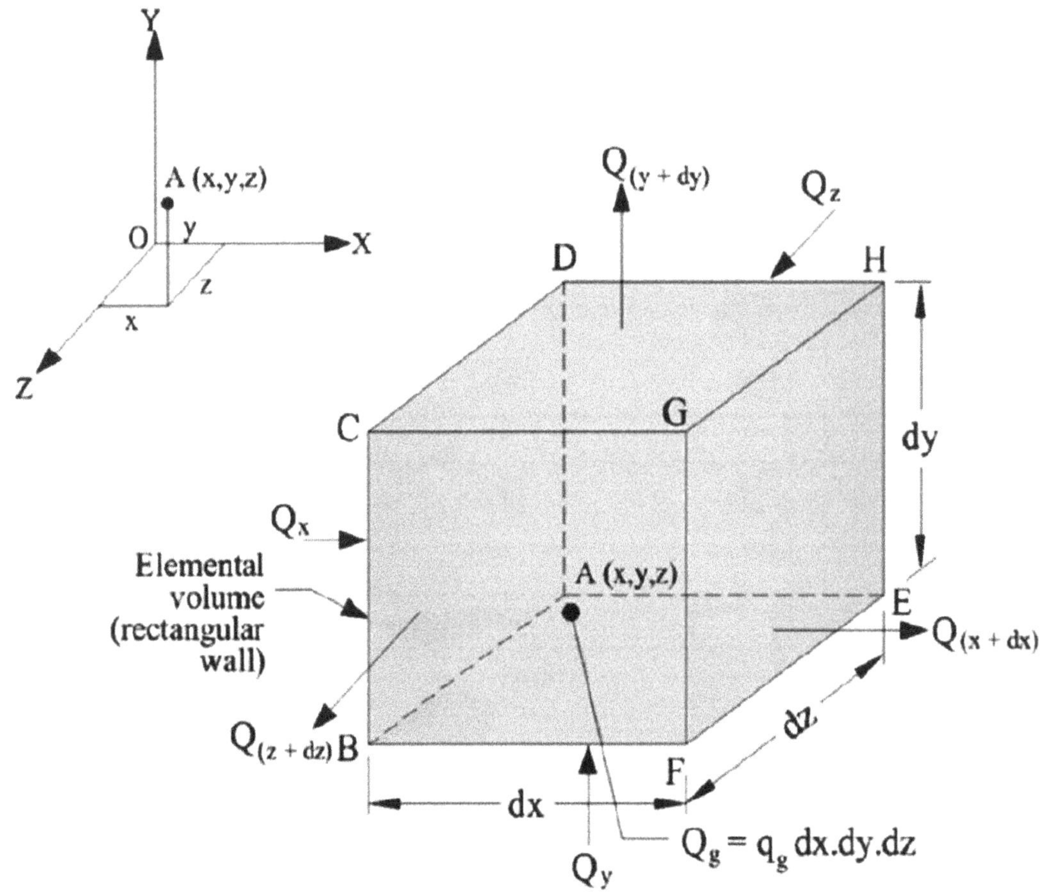

Figure 5 : Elemental volume in cartesian coordinate system

Let $Q' = Q(d\tau)$

= Total heat flow in the given direction for a small given value of time $(d\tau)$;

The unit of Q' will become kJ.

A. Net heat accumulated in the element due to conduction of heat from all the directions:

Assume Q'_x = total heat flow in the x-direction from the left side of the rectangular wall (i.e. face $ABCD$) in the time interval $d\tau$ (also known as heat influx). In the same way $Q'_{(x+dx)}$ is heat efflux heat coming out from face EFGH. The value of Q'_x and $Q'_{(x+dx)}$ are obtained as follows :

Heat influx, (from the left face of the wall ABCD)

$$Q'_x = -k_x (dy \cdot dz)\frac{\partial t}{\partial x} \cdot d\tau \quad \text{(According to Fourier's law, refer art 2.1)} \qquad ...(6)$$

The heat flowing out of the right face of the wall ($EFGH$) will be :

Heat efflux,

$$Q'_{(x+dx)} = Q'_x + \frac{\partial}{\partial x}(Q'_x)\,dx \qquad ...(7)$$

$\therefore$ Total heat accumulation in the X-direction (dQ'_x),

$$dQ'_x = Q'_x - \left[Q'_x + \frac{\partial}{\partial x}(Q'_x)\,dx \right]$$

$$= -\frac{\partial}{\partial x}(Q'_x)\,dx$$

$$= -\frac{\partial}{\partial x}\left[-k_x (dy.dz)\frac{\partial t}{\partial x} \cdot d\tau \right]dx$$

$$dQ'_x = \frac{\partial}{\partial x}\left[k_x \frac{\partial t}{\partial x} \right]dx.dy.dz.d\tau \qquad ...(8)$$

Similarly, the heat accumulated along Y and Z directions in time $d\tau$ will be :

$$dQ'_y = \frac{\partial}{\partial y}\left[k_y \frac{\partial t}{\partial y} \right]dx.dy.dz.d\tau \qquad ...(9)$$

$$dQ'_z = \frac{\partial}{\partial z}\left[k_z \frac{\partial t}{\partial z} \right]dx.dy.dz.d\tau \qquad ...(10)$$

$\therefore$ Net heat accumulated in the wall from all the coordinate directions considered will be :

$$= \frac{\partial}{\partial x}\left[k_x \frac{\partial t}{\partial x} \right]dx.dy.dz.d\tau + \frac{\partial}{\partial y}\left[k_y \frac{\partial t}{\partial y} \right]dx.dy.dz.d\tau + \frac{\partial}{\partial z}\left[k_z \frac{\partial t}{\partial z} \right]dx.dy.dz.d\tau$$

$$A = \left[\frac{\partial}{\partial x}\left(k_x \frac{\partial t}{\partial x} \right) + \frac{\partial}{\partial y}\left(k_y \frac{\partial t}{\partial y} \right) + \frac{\partial}{\partial z}\left(k_z \frac{\partial t}{\partial z} \right) \right]dx.dy.dz.d\tau \qquad ...(11)$$

B. Total heat generated within the wall $\left(Q'_g\right)$:

The total heat generated in the wall is given by

$$B = Q'_g = \dot{q}_g \left(dx.dy.dz\right)d\tau \qquad \text{...(12)}$$

[Following are some examples where alongwith heat transfer, heat is generated into the system :

a) curing of cement, b) electrical conductors, wires, c) combustion process,

d) fuel rods of nuclear reactors, etc.,]

C. Energy stored in the wall :

The total heat accumulated in the wall (eqn. 11) and the heat generated within the element (eqn. 12) together serve to increase the thermal energy of the wall. The increase in thermal energy is given by,

$$C = \rho \left(dx.dy.dz\right)c.\frac{\partial t}{\partial \tau} \cdot d\tau \qquad \text{...(13)}$$

[$\because$ Heat stored in the body = Mass of the body x specific heat of the body material x rise in the temperature of body]

Now, substituting eqns. (11), (12), (13) in the eqn. (5), we get

$$\left[\frac{\partial}{\partial x}\left(k_x\frac{\partial t}{\partial x}\right)+\frac{\partial}{\partial y}\left(k_y\frac{\partial t}{\partial y}\right)+\frac{\partial}{\partial z}\left(k_z\frac{\partial t}{\partial z}\right)\right]dx.dy.dz.d\tau + \dot{q}_g\left(dx.dy.dz\right)d\tau = \partial\left(dx.dy.dz\right)c.\frac{\partial t}{\partial \tau}.d\tau$$

Dividing both sides by $dx.dy.dz.d\tau$, we have

$$\frac{\partial}{\partial x}\left(k_x\frac{\partial t}{\partial x}\right)+\frac{\partial}{\partial y}\left(k_y\frac{\partial t}{\partial y}\right)+\frac{\partial}{\partial z}\left(k_z\frac{\partial t}{\partial z}\right)+\dot{q}_g = \rho.c.\frac{\partial t}{\partial \tau} \qquad \text{...(14)}$$

or, using the **vector operator** ∇ , we get

$$\nabla.\left(k\nabla t\right)+\dot{q}_g = \rho.c.\frac{\partial t}{\partial \tau} \qquad \text{...(15)}$$

This is known as the general heat conduction equation for 'non-homogeneous anisotropic material', 'Self heat generating' and 'unsteady three-dimensional heat flow.'

Q.2 **A) Derive the formula for the critical radius of insulation for a spherical object. Why does the rate of heat transfer initially decrease with insulation and then increase?**

- When the insulation thickness is less than the critical radius, adding insulation increases the surface area more than it increases resistance. So, heat loss increases.
- When the insulation thickness is greater than the critical radius, the conduction resistance becomes dominant, and heat loss decreases.

Thus, the rate of heat transfer initially increases, reaches a maximum at the critical radius, and then decreases with further insulation.

Consider a hollow sphere of outer radius r_1 is covered with a layer of insulation with outer radius r_2 having constant thermal conductivity k. The sphere is exposed to environment where air is at temperature of t_{air} and h_{air} is convection heat transfer coefficient for air. ($h_o = h_{air}$). Refer figure 19.

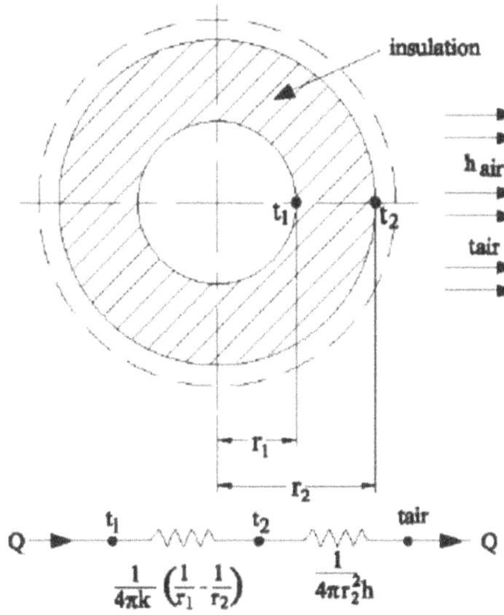

Figure 19 : Sphere with insulation

The heat flow rate can be expressed as :

$$Q = \frac{\left(t_1 - t_{air}\right)}{\dfrac{1}{4\pi k}\left(\dfrac{1}{r_1} - \dfrac{1}{r_2}\right) + \dfrac{1}{4\pi r_2^2 \cdot h}}$$

Adopting the same procedure as that of a cylinder, we have

$$\frac{dQ}{dr_2} = 0$$

$$\therefore \frac{d}{dr_2}\left[\frac{1}{4\pi k}\left(\frac{1}{r_1} - \frac{1}{r_2}\right) + \frac{1}{4\pi r_2^2 \cdot h_o}\right] = 0$$

$$\therefore \frac{1}{k \cdot r_2^2} - \frac{2}{r_2^3 \cdot h_o} = 0$$

$$\therefore r_2 = r_c = \text{critical radius of sphere} = \frac{2k}{h_o}$$

B   What are applications of heat exchangers? Classify heat exchangers.

Heat exchangers are devices used to transfer heat between two or more fluids without mixing them. They are widely used in various industries. Common applications include:

1. Power Plants – To transfer heat from steam or gases to water in boilers and condensers.
2. Refrigeration and Air Conditioning – Used in evaporators and condensers to transfer heat.
3. Automobiles – Radiators and oil coolers help maintain engine temperature.
4. Chemical Industries – For heating or cooling process fluids.

5. Food Processing – Used to pasteurize milk or juices and maintain product quality.
6. Petroleum Refineries – Used in distillation processes and heat recovery systems.

Heat exchangers can be classified in several ways:

1. Based on the Nature of Heat Exchange Process:
   - Direct Contact Type – Fluids come in direct contact (e.g., cooling towers).
   - Indirect Contact Type – Fluids are separated by a solid wall (e.g., shell and tube).

2. Based on Flow Arrangement:
   - Parallel Flow – Both fluids move in the same direction.
   - Counter Flow – Fluids move in opposite directions (more efficient).
   - Cross Flow – Fluids move perpendicular to each other.

3. Based on Construction:
   - Shell and Tube Heat Exchanger – One fluid flows through tubes, the other around them in a shell.
   - Plate Heat Exchanger – Fluids flow between thin plates, allowing compact design.
   - Fin Type Heat Exchanger – Fins increase surface area for heat transfer.

4. Based on Heat Transfer Mechanism:
   - Single-phase Heat Exchangers – Fluids remain in the same phase (liquid or gas).
   - Two-phase Heat Exchangers – One or both fluids change phase (e.g., boiling or condensation).

C **What are compact heat exchangers, Discuss the design and construction features of compact heat exchangers.**

Compact heat exchangers are special types of heat exchangers designed to provide a large heat transfer area within a small volume. These are used when space is limited and efficient heat transfer is required. They are especially useful when at least one of the fluids is a gas, which typically has low heat transfer capability.

Key Features of Compact Heat Exchangers:
   - High Surface Area to Volume Ratio: Compact heat exchangers typically have a surface area to volume ratio greater than $700 \ m^2/m^3$. This allows effective heat exchange even in small spaces.
   - Close Spacing of Flow Passages: The design includes narrow channels or passages to bring the fluids in close contact with large surface areas.
   - High Heat Transfer Efficiency: The compact design increases the rate of heat transfer and reduces the size of the equipment.

Design and Construction Features:
1. Surface Geometry:
   - Uses fins, corrugated plates, or micro-channels to increase surface area.
   - Surfaces may be wavy, louvered, or dimpled to enhance turbulence and heat transfer.
2. Flow Arrangement:
   - Fluids may flow in counterflow, crossflow, or parallel flow configurations.
   - Many compact exchangers use multi-pass designs for better thermal performance.
3. Materials Used:
   - Made from metals like aluminium, stainless steel, or copper for good thermal conductivity.
   - In corrosive environments, titanium or special alloys are used.

4. Fabrication Techniques:
   - Constructed using methods like brazing, welding, or mechanical bonding to ensure leak-proof and strong joints.
   - Often manufactured as a block or module with many thin plates or channels stacked together.
5. Compactness:
   - Suitable for automobiles, aircraft, HVAC systems, and electronic cooling, where size and weight are critical.
6. Types of Compact Heat Exchangers:
   - Plate-fin type
   - Tube-fin type
   - Printed circuit heat exchangers
   - Microchannel heat exchangers

Advantages:
- Small size and lightweight
- High heat transfer rate
- Low fluid inventory
- Quick response to temperature changes

Disadvantages:
- Higher manufacturing cost
- Difficult to clean and maintain
- Sensitive to fouling and clogging

OR

C **With usual notations derive the expression for effectiveness for a parallel flow heat exchanger.**

The heat exchange dQ through an area dA of the heat exchanger is given by

$$dQ = U.dA\left(t_h - t_c\right) \qquad \text{...(i)}$$

$$= -\dot{m}_h C_{p_h}\, dt_h = \dot{m}_c C_{pc}\, dt_c$$

$$= -C_h.dt_h = C_c.dt_c \qquad \text{...(ii) Refer figure no. 12}$$

From expression (ii), we can say,

$$dt_h = \frac{-dQ}{C_h} \quad \text{and} \quad dt_c = \frac{dQ}{C_c}$$

or

$$d\left(t_h - t_c\right) = -dQ\left[\frac{1}{C_h} + \frac{1}{C_c}\right]$$

Substituting the value of dQ from expression (i) and rearranging the equation, we get

$$\frac{d\left(t_h - t_c\right)}{\left(t_h - t_c\right)} = -U.dA\left[\frac{1}{C_h} + \frac{1}{C_c}\right]$$

By integrating above equation, we have

$$\ln\left[\frac{\left(t_{h2} - t_{c2}\right)}{\left(t_{h1} - t_{c1}\right)}\right] = -UA\left[\frac{1}{C_h} + \frac{1}{C_c}\right]$$

$$\therefore \ln\left[\frac{(t_{h2}-t_{c2})}{(t_{h1}-t_{c1})}\right] = -\frac{UA}{C_h}\left(1+\frac{C_h}{C_c}\right)$$

So, $\left(\dfrac{t_{h2}-t_{c2}}{t_{h1}-t_{c1}}\right) = \exp\left[-(UA/C_h)\{1+(C_h/C_c)\}\right]$ ...(32)

From equation 32, we have the expressions for effectiveness

$$\varepsilon = \frac{C_h\left(t_{h1}-t_{h2}\right)}{C_{\min}\left(t_{h1}-t_{c1}\right)} = \frac{C_c\left(t_{c2}-t_{c1}\right)}{C_{\min}\left(t_{h1}-t_{c1}\right)}$$

Hence, $t_{h2} = -\dfrac{\varepsilon C_{\min}\left(t_{h1}-t_{c1}\right)}{C_h} + t_{h1}$

$$t_{c2} = \frac{\varepsilon\, C_{\min}\left(t_{h1}-t_{c1}\right)}{C_c} + t_{c1}$$

Eliminating t_{h2} and t_{c2} from equation 32, with the help of above equations,

$$\frac{1}{\left(t_{h1}-t_{c1}\right)}\left[\left(t_{h1}-t_{c1}\right)-\varepsilon C_{\min}\left(t_{h1}-t_{c1}\right)\left(\frac{1}{C_h}+\frac{1}{C_c}\right)\right] = \exp\left[-(UA/C_h)\{1+C_h/C_c\}\right]$$

$$\therefore 1-\varepsilon\, C_{\min}\left(\frac{1}{C_h}+\frac{1}{C_c}\right) = \exp\left[-(UA/C_h)\{1+C_h/C_c\}\right]$$

So, $\varepsilon = \dfrac{1-\exp\left[-(UA/C_h)\{1+C_h/C_c\}\right]}{C_{\min}\left(\dfrac{1}{C_h}+\dfrac{1}{C_c}\right)}$ ...(33)

If $C_c < C_h$ then $C_{\min}=C_c$ and $C_{\max}=C_h$, hence eqn. 33 becomes

$$\varepsilon = \frac{1-\exp\left[-(UA/C_{\max})\{1+C_{\max}/C_{\min}\}\right]}{1+\left(C_{\min}/C_{\max}\right)}$$ ...(34)

If $C_h < C_c$ then $C_{\min}=C_h$ and $C_{\max}=C_c$, hence eqn. 33 becomes

$$\varepsilon = \frac{1-\exp\left[-(UA/C_{\min})\{1+C_{\min}/C_{\max}\}\right]}{1+\left(C_{\min}/C_{\max}\right)}$$ ...(35)

By rearranging eqns. 34 and 35, we get a common equation

$$\varepsilon = \frac{1-\exp\left[-(UA/C_{\min})\{1+C_{\min}/C_{\max}\}\right]}{1+\left(C_{\min}/C_{\max}\right)}$$ ...(36)

Q.3 A) Define the Biot number and explain its significance in determining the applicability of the lumped capacitance method.

The Biot number (Bi) is a dimensionless quantity used in heat transfer calculations. It compares the internal thermal resistance within a solid to the external thermal resistance between the solid's surface and the surrounding fluid.

The Biot number helps determine whether the lumped capacitance method can be used for transient heat conduction problems.

- If Bi < 0.1: The temperature inside the solid is nearly uniform at any instant. This means internal conduction is much faster than external convection. So, the lumped capacitance method is valid.
- If Bi > 0.1: There is a significant temperature gradient inside the solid. In this case, internal resistance cannot be neglected, and the lumped method is not accurate.

B	**What are fins, and why are they used in heat transfer applications? What are the advantages and limitations of using fins for heat transfer enhancement?**

Fins are extended surfaces attached to a solid object to increase the area available for heat transfer. They are usually made of materials with high thermal conductivity like aluminum or copper. Fins help transfer more heat from a surface to the surrounding fluid, especially when the surface area is limited.

Fins are extended surfaces attached to a solid object to increase the area available for heat transfer. They are usually made of materials with high thermal conductivity like aluminum or copper. Fins help transfer more heat from a surface to the surrounding fluid, especially when the surface area is limited.

Advantages of Using Fins:

1. Increased Heat Transfer Rate: Fins significantly increase the surface area, improving the rate of heat dissipation.
2. Compact Design: Effective heat removal allows for smaller, more compact systems.
3. Cost-Effective: Enhancing heat transfer through fins can be cheaper than using fans or pumps.
4. Passive Operation: Fins operate without external energy input, making them energy-efficient.

Limitations of Using Fins:

1. Added Weight and Volume: Fins increase the size and weight of the system, which may not be desirable in compact designs.
2. Material and Manufacturing Costs: High-conductivity materials and complex shapes may increase cost.
3. Reduced Effectiveness at High h Values: In fluids with high convection coefficients (like liquids), fins provide limited improvement.
4. Maintenance Issues: Fins may collect dust or corrosion over time, reducing effectiveness and requiring cleaning.

C	**Derive the expression for temperature distribution and heat transfer rate for a fin insulated at the tip.**

For above case, the boundary conditions are :

(i)	$x = 0, \theta = \theta_0$ and

(ii)	$x = L, \dfrac{dt}{dx} = 0$ ($\because$ temperature gradient at fin tip is zero.)

Applying the above conditions to the most general governing equation of fin, we have

$$\theta = c_1 \cdot e^{mx} + c_2 \cdot e^{-mx}$$

$$\therefore \theta_0 = c_1 + c_2 \qquad \text{...(a) (by applying first boundary condition)}$$

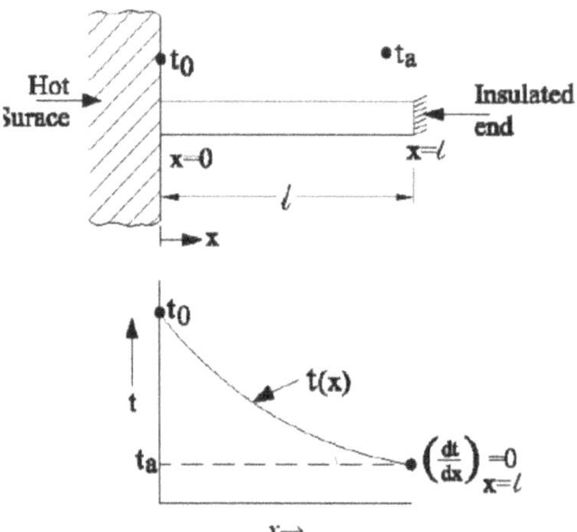

Figure 23 : Fin insulated from tip (case-2)

and

$$\theta = \left(t - t_a\right) = c_1 \cdot e^{mx} + c_2 e^{-mx}$$

$$\therefore \frac{dt}{dx} = m \cdot c_1 \cdot e^{mx} + (-m) c_2 \cdot e^{-mx}$$

by applying second boundary condition, we have

$$\left(\frac{dt}{dx}\right)_{x=L} = m \cdot c_1 \cdot e^{mL} - m \cdot c_2 \cdot e^{-mL} = 0$$

$$\therefore c_1 \cdot e^{mL} - c_2 \cdot e^{-mL} = 0 \qquad \qquad ...(b)$$

Solving equation (1) and (2), we have

$$c_2 = \theta_0 - c_1$$

Put the value of c_2 in equation (b), we have

$$c_1 \cdot e^{mL} - \left(\theta_0 - c_1\right) e^{-m \cdot L} = 0$$

$$\therefore c_1 \cdot e^{mL} - \theta_0 \cdot e^{-m \cdot L} + c_1 \cdot e^{-mL} = 0$$

$$\therefore c_1 \left(e^{mL} + e^{-mL}\right) = \theta_0 \cdot e^{-mL}$$

$$\therefore c_1 = \theta_0 \left[\frac{e^{-mL}}{e^{mL} + e^{-mL}}\right] \qquad \qquad ...(c)$$

and $c_2 = \theta_0 - c_1$

$$= \theta_0 - \theta_0 \left[\frac{e^{-mL}}{e^{mL} + e^{-mL}}\right]$$

$$c_2 = \theta_0 \left[1 - \frac{e^{-mL}}{e^{mL} + e^{-mL}}\right] = \theta_0 \left[\frac{e^{mL}}{e^{mL} + e^{-mL}}\right] \qquad ...(d)$$

By substituting the values of c_1 and c_2 in the most general equation of heat dissipation from the fin. We have

$$\theta = \theta_0 \left[\frac{e^{-mL}}{e^{mL} + e^{-mL}} \right] e^{mx} + \theta_0 \left[\frac{e^{mL}}{e^{mL} + e^{-mL}} \right] e^{-mx}$$

$$\therefore \frac{\theta}{\theta_0} = \frac{e^{m(L-x)} + e^{-m(L-x)}}{e^{mL} + e^{-mL}}$$

$$\therefore \frac{t - t_a}{t_0 - t_a} = \frac{\theta}{\theta_0} = \frac{\cosh\{m(L-x)\}}{\cosh(mL)} \qquad \text{...(e)}$$

Equation (e) represents the equation for temperature distribution for a finite fin having insulated tip.

Now,

The rate of heat dissipation from the fin is given by

$$Q_{fin} = -k \cdot A_{cs} \left(\frac{dt}{dx} \right)_{x=0} \qquad \text{...(f)}$$

from equation (e), we have

$$(t - t_a) = (t_o - t_a) \left[\frac{\cosh\{m(L-x)\}}{\cosh(mL)} \right]$$

$$\therefore \left(\frac{dt}{dx} \right)_{x=0} = (t_o - t_a)\left[(-m)\right]\left[\frac{\cosh\{m(L-x)\}}{\cosh(mL)} \right]$$

$$= (t_o - t_a)(-m)\left[\frac{\sinh(mL)}{\cosh(mL)} \right]$$

$$\left(\frac{dt}{dx} \right)_{x=0} = -m(t_o - t_a) \cdot \tanh(mL)$$

By substituting the above value in equation (f),

$$\therefore Q_{fin} = k \cdot A_{cs} \cdot m \cdot (t_o - t_a) \cdot \tanh(m \cdot L)$$

$$Q_{fin} = \sqrt{p \cdot h \cdot A_{cs} \cdot k}\,(t_o - t_a) \cdot \tanh(m \cdot L) \qquad \text{...(g)}$$

OR

Q.3 A) Differentiate fin efficiency and fin effectiveness.

Fin Efficiency	Fin Effectiveness
Fin efficiency is the ratio of actual heat transfer by the fin to the heat transfer if the entire fin were at the base temperature.	Fin effectiveness is the ratio of heat transfer with the fin to the heat transfer without the fin (from the base surface only).
Measures how well the fin material and design utilize its surface to transfer heat.	Measures whether the fin is beneficial in increasing heat transfer.
Always less than or equal to 1.	Usually greater than 1 (fin is useful if effectiveness > 1).

Quality of heat transfer through the fin.	Whether using a fin is advantageous in a particular situation.

B **What is a thermometer well, and why are errors introduced during temperature measurements?**

A thermometer well (also called a thermowell) is a protective metal tube that is inserted into a process fluid to hold a temperature sensor like a thermometer or thermocouple. It allows temperature measurement without directly exposing the sensor to the fluid. This protects the sensor from corrosion, pressure, and flow damage, and also makes it easier to replace or maintain the sensor without stopping the process.

When a thermometer well is used, the temperature reading may not be exactly the same as the actual fluid temperature. This happens due to the following reasons:

1. Heat Conduction Along the Well: Heat can flow from the fluid through the well and along its length toward the cooler surroundings. This lowers the temperature at the sensor tip, causing an error.
2. Thermal Resistance Between Well and Sensor: If the sensor is not in perfect contact with the inner surface of the well, there may be an air gap. This adds thermal resistance and delays heat transfer, reducing accuracy.
3. Low Fluid Velocity: If the fluid around the well is moving slowly, the heat transfer is poor, and the well may not reach the actual fluid temperature quickly or accurately.
4. Well Material and Thickness: The thermal conductivity and thickness of the well affect how quickly it responds to temperature changes. A thick or low-conductivity well can delay or reduce heat transfer to the sensor.

C **With usual notations derive the generalized heat conduction equation in spherical coordinates and explain its specific applications.**

While dealing with problems of heat conduction having spherical geometry (i.e. in liquid gas spherical storage tanks, spherical vessels in chemical units, dome of nuclear power plant (hemi-spherical shape), it is convenient to use spherical coordinate system.

Consider an elemental volume having the coordinates (r, ϕ, θ), for three dimensional heat conduction analysis, as shown in figure 07.

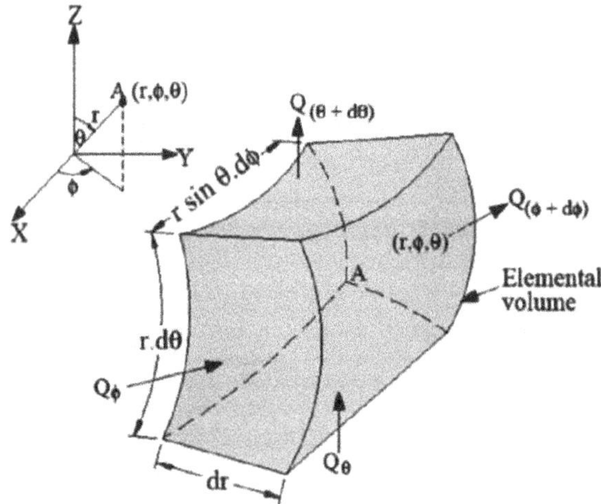

Figure 7 : Elemental volume in spherical coordinate system

Let heat accumulated in the sphere due to conduction of heat :

– Heat flow through $r-\theta$ plane: ϕ-direction :

Heat influx, $Q'_\phi = -k\,(\,dr.rd\theta\,)\dfrac{\partial t}{r.\sin\theta.\partial\phi}\,d\tau$

Heat efflux, $Q'_{(\phi+d\phi)} = Q'_\phi + \dfrac{\partial}{r.\sin\theta.\partial\phi}(Q'_\phi)\,r\sin\theta.d\phi$

$\therefore$ Heat accumulated in the ϕ-direction,

$$dQ'_\phi = Q'_\phi - Q'_{(\phi+d\phi)}$$

$$= \dfrac{-\partial}{r\sin\theta\cdot\partial\phi}(Q'_\phi)\,r\sin\theta.d\phi$$

$$= -\dfrac{1}{r\sin\theta}\cdot\dfrac{\partial}{\partial\phi}\left[-k\,(\,dr.rd\theta\,)\dfrac{1}{r\sin\theta}\cdot\dfrac{\partial t}{\partial\phi}\cdot\partial\tau\right]r\sin\theta.d\phi$$

$$dQ'_\phi = k\,(\,dr.rd\theta.r\sin\theta.d\phi\,)\dfrac{1}{r^2\sin^2\theta}\cdot\dfrac{\partial^2 t}{\partial\phi^2}\,d\tau \qquad\qquad …(41)$$

– Heat flow in $r-\phi$ plane, θ-direction :

Heat influx, $Q'_\theta = -k\,(\,dr.r\sin\theta.d\phi\,)\dfrac{\partial t}{r\partial\theta}\cdot d\tau$

Heat efflux, $Q'_{(\theta+d\theta)} = Q'_\theta + \dfrac{\partial}{r\partial\theta}(Q'_\theta)\,rd\theta$

$\therefore$ Heat accumulated in the θ-direction,

$$dQ'_\theta = Q'_\theta - Q'_{(\theta+d\theta)}$$

$$= -\dfrac{\partial}{r.\partial\theta}(Q'_\theta)\,r.d\theta$$

$$dQ'_\theta = -\dfrac{\partial}{r.\partial\theta}\left[-k\,(\,dr.r\sin\theta.d\phi\,)\dfrac{\partial t}{r\partial\theta}\cdot d\tau\right]r.d\theta \qquad\qquad …(42)$$

$$\therefore dQ'_\theta = k\,(\,dr.rd\theta.r\sin\theta.d\phi\,)\dfrac{1}{r^2\sin\theta}\cdot\dfrac{\partial}{\partial\theta}\left[\sin\theta\cdot\dfrac{\partial t}{\partial\theta}\right]d\tau \qquad\qquad …(43)$$

– Heat flow in $\theta-\phi$ plane, r-direction :

Heat influx, $Q'_r = -k\,(\,rd\theta.r\sin\theta.d\phi\,)\dfrac{\partial t}{\partial r}\cdot\partial\tau$

Heat efflux, $Q'_{(r+rd)} = Q'_r + \dfrac{\partial}{\partial r}(Q'_r)\,dr$

$\therefore$ Heat accumulation in the r-direction,

$$dQ'_r = Q'_r - Q'_{(r+dr)}$$

$$= -\frac{\partial}{\partial r}(Q'_r)\,dr$$

$$= -\frac{\partial}{\partial r}\left[-k\,(rd\theta.r\sin\theta.d\phi)\frac{\partial t}{\partial r}\cdot d\tau\right]dr$$

$$= kd\theta.\sin\theta.d\phi dr\,\frac{\partial}{\partial r}\left[r^2\cdot\frac{\partial t}{\partial r}\right]d\tau$$

$$dQ'_r = k\,(dr.rd\theta.r\sin\theta.d\phi)\frac{1}{r^2}\cdot\frac{\partial}{\partial r}\left[r^2\cdot\frac{\partial t}{\partial r}\right]d\tau \qquad \text{...(44)}$$

Net heat accumulated in the sphere.

$$A = k.dr.rd\theta.r\sin\theta.d\phi\left[\frac{1}{r^2\sin^2\theta}\cdot\frac{\partial^2 t}{\partial\phi^2}+\frac{1}{r^2\sin\phi}\cdot\frac{\partial}{\partial\theta}\left(\sin\theta\cdot\frac{\partial t}{\partial\theta}\right)+\frac{1}{r^2}\cdot\frac{\partial}{\partial r}\left(r^2\cdot\frac{\partial t}{\partial r}\right)\right]d\tau$$

$$\text{...(45)}$$

B. Heat generated within the element $\left(Q'_g\right)$:

The total heat generated within the element is given by,

$$B = Q'_g = \dot{q}_g\,(dr.rd\phi.r\sin\theta.d\phi)\,d\tau \qquad \text{...(46)}$$

C. Energy stored in the element :

The increase in thermal energy in the element is equal to

$$C = \rho\,(dr.rd\theta.r\sin\theta.d\phi)\,c.\frac{\partial t}{\partial\tau}.d\tau \qquad \text{...(47)}$$

Now, (A) + (B) = (C)   ... Energy balance

$$\therefore kdr.rd\theta.r\sin\theta.d\phi\left[\frac{1}{r^2\sin^2\theta}\cdot\frac{\partial^2 t}{\partial\phi^2}+\frac{1}{r^2\sin\theta}\cdot\frac{\partial}{\partial\theta}\left(\sin\theta\cdot\frac{\partial t}{\partial\theta}\right)+\frac{1}{r^2}\cdot\frac{\partial}{\partial r}\left(r^2\cdot\frac{\partial t}{\partial r}\right)\right]\cdot d\tau$$

$$+\dot{q}_g\,(dr.rd\theta.r\sin\theta.d\phi)\,d\tau = \rho\,(dr.rd\theta.r\sin\theta.d\phi)\,c.\frac{\partial t}{\partial\tau}.d\tau \qquad \text{...(48)}$$

Dividing both sides by $k.(dr.rd\theta.r\sin\theta.d\phi)\,d\tau$ to equation (48) we get

$$\left[\frac{1}{r^2\sin^2\theta}\cdot\frac{\partial^2 t}{\partial\phi^2}+\frac{1}{r^2\sin\theta}\cdot\frac{\partial}{\partial\theta}\left(\sin\theta\cdot\frac{\partial t}{\partial\theta}\right)+\frac{1}{r^2}\cdot\frac{\partial}{\partial r}\left(r^2\cdot\frac{\partial t}{\partial r}\right)\right]+\frac{q_g}{k}$$

$$= \frac{\rho c}{k}\cdot\frac{\partial t}{\partial\tau}=\frac{1}{\alpha}\cdot\frac{\partial t}{\partial\tau} \qquad \text{...(49)}$$

Equation (49) is the general heat conduction equation for isotropic material/homogeneous material with internal heat generation having unsteady state in spherical coordinate system.

Q.4 A) What are radiation shields, and how do they reduce heat transfer?

Radiation shields are thin, reflective surfaces placed between two objects to reduce the transfer of heat by thermal radiation. They work by reflecting a large part of the thermal radiation and reducing the amount of heat that passes from one surface to another.

These shields are typically made of materials with low emissivity (such as polished aluminium or stainless steel) and are used in applications where insulation from radiation heat transfer is important, such as in cryogenics, spacecraft, and thermal insulation systems.

Radiation heat transfer depends on the emissivity of the surfaces and the temperature difference between them. Radiation shields help reduce heat transfer in the following ways:

1. Reflecting Radiation: The shiny surface of the shield reflects much of the radiation back toward the source instead of allowing it to pass through.
2. Breaking the Radiation Path: By placing one or more shields between hot and cold surfaces, the direct view is blocked. Heat must now transfer through multiple layers, each with its own radiation loss.
3. Lower Effective Emissivity: With each additional shield, the net emissivity of the system decreases, which reduces the overall heat transfer.

B What is the Von-Karman integral momentum equation, Explain the physical significance of the terms in the Von-Karman equation.

The Von Kármán integral momentum equation is a simplified form of the boundary layer momentum equation. It is used to analyze the flow of a fluid over a flat surface, such as air over a flat plate. This equation helps estimate the boundary layer thickness, wall shear stress, and drag force without solving the full Navier–Stokes equations.

Physical Significance of the Terms:

1. Wall Shear Stress (τ_w): This represents the friction force per unit area exerted by the fluid on the surface. It is caused by the velocity gradient near the wall within the boundary layer.
2. Fluid Density (ρ): Density affects how much momentum the fluid has. A higher density means more mass is involved in the flow, which influences the shear force.
3. Free Stream Velocity ($U\infty$): This is the velocity of the fluid outside the boundary layer (undisturbed flow). It is a reference for comparing how the boundary layer slows down the fluid near the wall.
4. Momentum Thickness (θ): This term measures the loss of momentum due to the development of the boundary layer. It shows how much the velocity of the flow has decreased because of friction.
5. Rate of Change of Momentum Thickness ($d\theta/dx$): This tells how fast the momentum thickness is growing as the flow moves along the surface. A faster growth means the boundary layer is thickening more quickly, which increases shear stress.

C Define the following dimensionless numbers and explain their physical significance: Reynolds number (Re), Nusselt number (Nu), Prandtl number (Pr), Grashoff number (Gr), Peclet number (Pe), Biot number (Bi).

The Reynolds number (Re) is the ratio of inertial forces to viscous forces in a fluid flow.

Re=Inertial Forces/Viscous Forces

It indicates whether the fluid flow is laminar or turbulent.

- Low Re (< 2000): Laminar flow
- High Re (> 4000): Turbulent flow

- Transition occurs between these values.

The Nusselt number (Nu) is the ratio of convective heat transfer to conductive heat transfer across a boundary (such as a solid surface).

Nu=Convective Heat Transfer/Conductive Heat Transfer

It shows how effectively heat is transferred by convection compared to conduction.

- Nu = 1: Pure conduction
- Nu > 1: Enhanced heat transfers due to convection

The Prandtl number (Pr) is the ratio of momentum diffusivity to thermal diffusivity.

Pr=Momentum Diffusivity/Thermal Diffusivity

It compares how fast momentum and heat are transported in a fluid.

- Low Pr (< 1): Heat diffuses faster (e.g., liquid metals)
- High Pr (> 1): Momentum diffuses faster (e.g., oils)

The Grashoff number (Gr) is the ratio of buoyancy force to viscous force in a fluid.

Gr=Buoyancy Force/Viscous Force

It predicts the strength of natural convection in a fluid.

- High Gr: Strong natural convection
- Low Gr: Weak or negligible natural convection

The Peclet number (Pe) is the ratio of convective heat transfer to conductive (or diffusive) heat transfer in a fluid.

Pe=Convective Heat Transfer/ Conductive (Diffusive) Heat Transfer

It shows whether heat transfer is dominated by fluid motion or by molecular diffusion.

- High Pe: Convection dominates
- Low Pe: Conduction dominates

The Biot number (Bi) is the ratio of internal thermal resistance within a solid to the external thermal resistance due to convection.

Bi=Conduction Resistance (inside solid)/Convection Resistance (at surface)

It determines if temperature inside a solid can be considered uniform.

- Bi < 0.1: Lumped system assumption is valid
- Bi > 0.1: Temperature gradients exist within the solid

OR

Q.4   A) Explain the physical significance of the momentum equation in fluid flow.

The momentum equation in fluid flow expresses the balance of forces acting on a fluid element. It is derived from Newton's second law of motion, which states that the rate of change of momentum equals the sum of forces applied. The Momentum Equation Tell Us;

1. Force and Motion Relationship: It shows how forces such as pressure, viscous (friction) forces, and body forces (like gravity) affect the fluid's velocity and acceleration.
2. Flow Behaviour Prediction: By solving the momentum equation, we can predict how a fluid will move under different conditions — for example, how it speeds up, slows down, or changes direction.
3. Role of Viscosity: The equation accounts for viscous forces, explaining how internal friction in the fluid resists motion and causes energy loss.
4. Pressure Effects: It includes pressure forces that drive the flow or resist it, helping understand phenomena like pressure drops in pipes.
5. Application to Engineering Problems: The momentum equation helps design equipment like pumps, turbines, and ventilation systems by modeling fluid behaviour accurately.

B   Outline the assumptions made in deriving the Blasius solution for a laminar boundary layer and describe the steps involved in solving the Blasius equation for boundary layer thickness.

Steps Involved in Solving the Blasius Equation for Boundary Layer Thickness

1. **Understanding the Blasius Equation:**

   The Blasius equation is a nonlinear ordinary differential equation used to describe the velocity profile of laminar boundary layer flow over a flat plate. It is expressed as:

   $$f''' + \frac{1}{2}ff'' = 0$$

   where f is a dimensionless stream function dependent on the similarity variable η.

2. **Define Similarity Variables:**

   Introduce the similarity variable η and the dimensionless stream function $f(\eta)$:

   $$\eta = y\sqrt{\frac{U_\infty}{\nu x}}, \quad \psi = \sqrt{\nu U_\infty x}\, f(\eta)$$

   Here, y is the distance normal to the plate, x is the distance along the plate, U_∞ is the free stream velocity, and ν is the kinematic viscosity.

3. **Apply Boundary Conditions:**

   The boundary conditions for the Blasius equation are:

   $$f(0) = 0, \quad f'(0) = 0, \quad f'(\infty) = 1$$

   These correspond to no velocity at the wall, no slip condition, and free stream velocity far from the plate.

4. **Convert to a System of First-Order ODEs:**

   To solve numerically, rewrite the third-order ODE as a system of three first-order ODEs:

   $$f_1 = f, \quad f_2 = f', \quad f_3 = f''$$

   Then:

   $$f_1' = f_2, \quad f_2' = f_3, \quad f_3' = -\frac{1}{2}f_1 f_3$$

5. **Numerical Solution:**

   Use numerical methods such as the Runge-Kutta method or shooting method to solve the system starting from $\eta = 0$. Because the boundary condition at infinity cannot be directly used, guess the initial value of $f''(0)$ and adjust it until $f'(\eta)$ approaches 1 as η becomes large.

6. **Calculate Boundary Layer Thickness:**

   After finding $f(\eta)$ and $f'(\eta)$, calculate the boundary layer thickness δ where the velocity reaches 99% of the free stream velocity:

   $$u = U_\infty f'(\eta), \quad \delta \approx \frac{5x}{\sqrt{Re_x}} \quad \text{where} \quad Re_x = \frac{U_\infty x}{\nu}$$

Assumptions Made in Deriving the Blasius Solution;
1. Steady Flow: The flow does not change with time.

2. Two-Dimensional Flow: Flow varies only along the surface (x-direction) and perpendicular to it (y-direction), ignoring variations in the third direction.

3. Incompressible Flow: Fluid density remains constant throughout.

4. Laminar Flow: The flow is smooth and orderly, with no turbulence.

5. Flat Plate with Zero Pressure Gradient: The flow is over a flat plate with no change in pressure along the surface.

C **Define the following terms: Reflectivity, transmissivity, Emissivity, Kirchhoff's law, Planck's law, Wien's law, Stefan- Boltzmann law.**

1. Reflectivity (ρ): The fraction of incident radiant energy that is reflected by a surface.

It shows how much energy bounces off a surface without being absorbed or transmitted.

2. Transmissivity (τ): The fraction of incident radiant energy that passes through a material.

It indicates how much radiation goes through the material without being absorbed or reflected.

3. Emissivity (ε): The ratio of radiation emitted by a surface to the radiation emitted by a perfect blackbody at the same temperature.

It measures how effectively a surface emits thermal radiation.

- o $\varepsilon=1$: perfect emitter (blackbody)
- o $\varepsilon=0$: perfect reflector (no emission)

4. Kirchhoff's Law: At thermal equilibrium, the emissivity of a surface equals its absorptivity for radiation at each wavelength.

A good absorber is also a good emitter at the same wavelength and temperature.

5. Planck's Law: It gives the spectral distribution of radiation emitted by a blackbody as a function of wavelength and temperature.

It describes how much energy a perfect emitter radiates at each wavelength depending on temperature.

6. Wien's Law: The wavelength at which the radiation emitted by a blackbody is maximum is inversely proportional to the temperature.

$$\lambda max=b/T \quad \text{where } b=2.898\times10^{-3}\,\text{m·K (Wien's displacement constant)}$$

Hotter objects emit peak radiation at shorter wavelengths (bluer light).

7. Stefan-Boltzmann Law: The total energy radiated per unit surface area of a blackbody is proportional to the fourth power of its absolute temperature.

$$E=\sigma T^4 \quad \text{where } \sigma=5.67\times10^{-8}\,\text{W/m}^2\text{K}^4 \text{ (Stefan-Boltzmann constant).}$$ As temperature increases, total emitted radiation rises rapidly.

Q.5 **A) What is a shape factor, and why is it important in radiation heat exchange?**

The shape factor (also called the view factor or configuration factor) is the fraction of radiation energy leaving one surface that directly reaches another surface.

It depends only on the geometry and orientation of the surfaces involved, and not on temperature or material properties.

Importance in Radiation Heat Exchange:

1. Determines Radiation Exchange: Shape factors help quantify how much radiative energy transfers between surfaces in an enclosure.

2. Simplifies Calculations: They allow the complex problem of radiative heat exchange in irregular shapes to be broken down using geometric relationships.

3. Used in Radiation Networks: Together with surface emissivity and temperatures, shape factors enable the calculation of net radiative heat transfer between multiple surfaces.

4. Energy Conservation: Shape factors satisfy the reciprocity and summation rules, ensuring energy balance in radiative heat transfer problems.

B   **Explain the significance of the overall heat transfer coefficient in heat exchanger analysis.**
The overall heat transfer coefficient (U) represents the combined effect of all modes of heat transfer—conduction, convection, and sometimes radiation—through the surfaces separating two fluids in a heat exchanger.

☐Simplifies Complex Heat Transfer: Instead of analysing each resistance separately (like fluid convection inside tubes, conduction through walls, and convection outside), the overall coefficient combines them into a single value.

☐Measures Heat Transfer Efficiency: A higher overall heat transfer coefficient means heat passes more easily from the hot fluid to the cold fluid, indicating a more efficient heat exchanger.

☐Used in Design and Performance: The overall coefficient is used in the fundamental heat exchanger equation. This helps determine the required size and design of heat exchangers.

☐ Helps Identify Bottlenecks: By calculating U, engineers can find which part of the heat transfer process (fluid convection or wall conduction) limits performance and improve it.

C   **Derive the expression for radiation heat exchange between two black bodies.**

- Two black bodies: Body 1 and Body 2.

- Temperatures: T_1 and T_2 (assume $T_1 > T_2$)

- Surface areas: A_1 and A_2

- View factors: F_{12} (fraction of radiation leaving surface 1 that hits surface 2), and F_{21}

- Both bodies are **black** (perfect absorbers and emitters).

The total radiant energy emitted by a black body per unit time from surface i is given by **Stefan-Boltzmann law**:

$$E_i = \sigma A_i T_i^4$$

where

- $\sigma = 5.67 \times 10^{-8}\,\mathrm{W/m^2K^4}$ (Stefan-Boltzmann constant)

The radiation leaving surface 1 that actually reaches surface 2 is:

$$Q_{1 \to 2} = E_1 F_{12} = \sigma A_1 T_1^4 F_{12}$$

Similarly, radiation leaving surface 2 that reaches surface 1 is:

$$Q_{2 \to 1} = \sigma A_2 T_2^4 F_{21}$$

Since both bodies are black (absorptivity = emissivity = 1), they absorb all incident radiation from each other.

Therefore, the **net radiation heat exchange** from body 1 to body 2 is:

$$Q_{net} = Q_{1 \to 2} - Q_{2 \to 1} = \sigma \left(A_1 T_1^4 F_{12} - A_2 T_2^4 F_{21} \right)$$

From radiative heat transfer theory, the view factors satisfy the **reciprocity relation**:

$$A_1 F_{12} = A_2 F_{21}$$

So,

$$Q_{net} = \sigma A_1 F_{12} \left(T_1^4 - T_2^4 \right)$$

$$Q_{\text{net}} = \sigma A_1 F_{12} \left(T_1^4 - T_2^4\right)$$

This expression gives the net radiation heat exchange from black body 1 to black body 2.

OR

Q.5 **A) Distinguish between the hydrodynamic and thermal boundary layers.**

Hydrodynamic Boundary Layer	Thermal Boundary Layer
Region near a solid surface where fluid velocity changes from zero (due to no-slip condition) to free stream velocity.	Region near a solid surface were fluid temperature changes from wall temperature to free stream temperature.
Viscosity of the fluid causing velocity gradients	Thermal conductivity and convection causing temperature gradients
Thickness over which velocity changes significantly	Thickness over which temperature changes significantly
Due to viscous forces resisting fluid motion near the surface	Due to heat transfer between solid surface and fluid
Affects fluid flow velocity and shear stress at the surface	Affects heat transfer rate between surface and fluid

B **What is the fouling factor, and how does it affect the performance of a heat exchanger?**
The fouling factor (often denoted as Rf) is a measure of the resistance to heat transfer caused by the accumulation of unwanted deposits—such as dirt, scale, corrosion products, biological growth, or other contaminants—on the heat transfer surfaces inside a heat exchanger.

☐ Decreases heat transfer rate: Fouling deposits act as an insulating layer, increasing thermal resistance and reducing the overall heat transfer coefficient (U).
☐ Increases temperature differences: More temperature difference is required to transfer the same amount of heat.
☐ Raises operating costs: Reduced heat exchanger efficiency leads to higher energy consumption (e.g., more pumping power or additional heating/cooling).
☐ Causes increased pressure drop: Fouling can also restrict flow, increasing pressure drop and energy needed for pumping.
☐ Shortens equipment life: Excessive fouling can cause corrosion or damage, reducing heat exchanger lifespan.

C **Define the overall heat transfer coefficient and derive its expression for a heat exchanger. How does the overall heat transfer coefficient vary for single-phase and two-phase heat transfer?**
The overall heat transfer coefficient (U) is a measure of the heat transfer capability across multiple resistances (conduction, convection, fouling, etc.) in a composite system like a heat exchanger.
It represents the total heat transfer rate per unit area per unit temperature difference between the two fluids separated by the heat transfer surface.

For prediction and designing the performance of heat exchanger, it is necessary to know various parameters related to it.

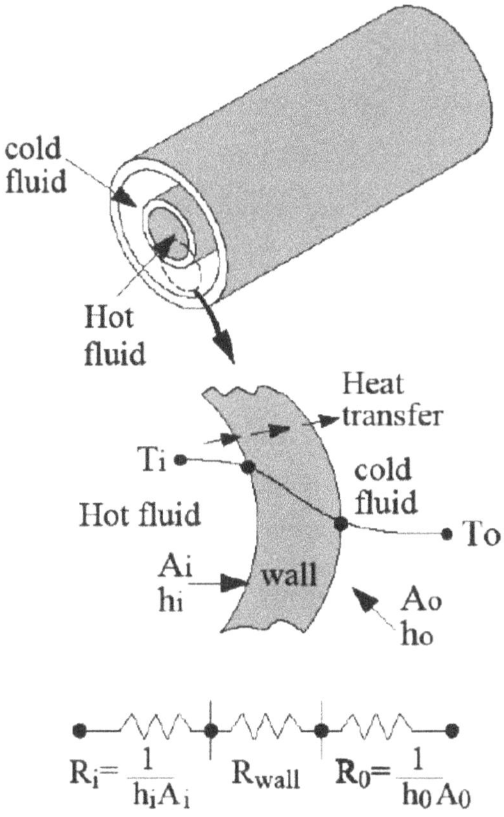

Figure 11 : Heat exchanger analysis with thermal circuit

Refer figure no. 11. It represents the flow of hot fluid through the hollow cylinder and cold fluid is surrounded to it. The cylinder wall possesses some value of thickness. The heat is flowing from inner side to outer side (i.e. from centre to surface. The resistance offered to the flow of fluids are (i) resistance offered due to convection (between hot fluid and inner layer of cylinder), (ii) resistance offered due to conduction (by cylinder wall material), (iii) resistance offered due to convection (by external layer of cylinder and colder fluid). The thermal circuit for the same is shown in figure 11.

$$Q = \frac{\Delta t}{R_{th}} = \frac{\Delta t}{\dfrac{1}{h_i A_i} + \dfrac{1}{2\pi KL}\ln\left(\dfrac{r_o}{r_i}\right) + \dfrac{1}{ho \cdot Ao}} = UA\Delta t = U_i \cdot A_i \cdot \Delta t = U_o \cdot A_o \cdot \Delta t \qquad ...(1)$$

where, U_i, U_o = internal and external value of overall heat transfer coefficient: $w/m^2 k$

r_o, r_i = outer and inner radii: m

$$\therefore Q = \frac{\Delta t}{R_{th}} = \frac{\Delta t}{1/UA} = \frac{\Delta t}{1/U_i \cdot A_i} = \frac{\Delta t}{1/U_o \cdot A_o} = \frac{\Delta t}{\dfrac{1}{h_i \cdot A_i} + \dfrac{1}{2\pi KL}\ln\left(\dfrac{r_o}{r_i}\right) + \dfrac{1}{ho \cdot Ao}}$$

$$\therefore \quad \frac{1}{\dfrac{1}{h_i \cdot A_i} + \dfrac{1}{h_o \cdot A_o} + \dfrac{1}{2\pi KL}\ln{}^{r_o}\!\!/_{r_i}} = U_o \cdot A_o$$

$$\therefore \quad \frac{A_o}{h_i \cdot A_i} + \frac{1}{h_o} + \frac{A_o}{2\pi KL}\ln{}^{r_o}\!\!/_{r_i} = \frac{1}{U_o} \qquad \qquad ...(2)$$

Similarly,

$$\therefore \quad \frac{1}{h_i} + \frac{A_i}{A_o \cdot h_o} + \frac{A_i}{2\pi KL}\ln{}^{r_o}\!\!/_{r_i} = \frac{1}{U_i} \qquad \qquad ...(3)$$

Variation of Overall Heat Transfer Coefficient for Single-Phase vs Two-Phase Heat Transfer:

☐ Single-phase heat transfer: Both fluids remain in a single phase (liquid or gas). Heat transfer coefficients h1 and h2 depend mainly on convection. These coefficients tend to be moderate and vary with fluid properties, flow velocity, turbulence, etc.

☐ Two-phase heat transfer: One of the fluids undergoes phase change (boiling or condensation). Phase change heat transfer coefficients are much higher than single-phase convective coefficients because latent heat transfer is involved, and the process is usually more effective.
- During boiling (liquid to vapor), h can be very large due to nucleate boiling.
- During condensation (vapor to liquid), h is high due to film or dropwise condensation.

PAPER 2_ 3151909: HEAT TRANSFER

WINTER 2024 EXAM   DATE: 28/11/2024

Q.1 **A) Distinguish between the conduction, convection and radiation modes of heat transfer with suitable example.**

1. Conduction: Conduction is the transfer of heat through a solid material from one molecule to another without any movement of the material as a whole. It occurs due to the vibration and interaction of particles in a solid.

Example: When a metal rod is heated at one end, the heat travels through the rod to the other end. If you touch the other end after a while, it becomes hot due to conduction.

2. Convection: Convection is the transfer of heat by the movement of a fluid (liquid or gas). It occurs when the warmer part of the fluid rises and the cooler part sinks, setting up a circulation pattern. Example: Boiling water in a pot: the water at the bottom gets heated, becomes less dense, rises, and cooler water descends to take its place, creating a convection current.

3. Radiation: Radiation is the transfer of heat in the form of electromagnetic waves (usually infrared), without needing any medium. It can occur even in a vacuum.

Example: The Sun heating the Earth: Heat travels through the vacuum of space via radiation.

B **Draw temperature variation for the condenser of the domestic refrigerator and evaporator of the thermal power plant.**

condenser of the domestic refrigerator   evaporator of the thermal power plant

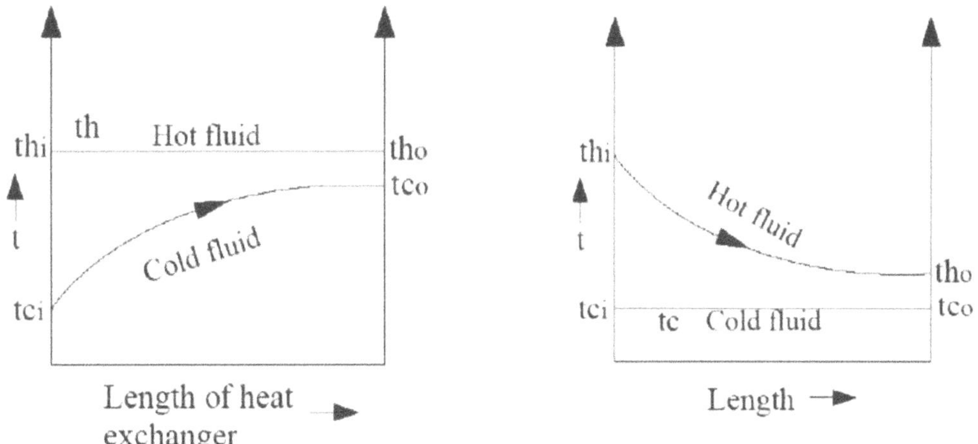

C **Derive equation of logarithmic mean temperature difference for parallel flow heat-exchanger.**

Let us consider an elementary area dA of the heat exchanger. The rate of flow of heat through this elementary area is given by (Refer figure no. 12)

$$dQ = UdA\left(t_h - t_c\right) = U \cdot dA \cdot \Delta t$$

As a result of heat transfer dQ through the area dA, the hot fluid is cooled by dt_h whereas the cold fluid is heated up by dt_c. The heat balance over a differential area dA,

$$dQ = -\dot{m}_h \cdot c_{ph} \cdot dt_h = \dot{m}_c \cdot c_{pc} \cdot dt_c = U \cdot dA\left(t_h - t_c\right) \qquad \ldots(5)$$

(where, dt_h is $-$ve and dt_c is $+$ve)

$$\text{So,} \quad dt_h = -\frac{dQ}{\dot{m}_h c_{ph}} = -\frac{dQ}{C_h}$$

$$\text{and,} \quad dt_c = \frac{dQ}{\dot{m}_c c_{pc}} = \frac{dQ}{C_c}$$

where, $\quad C_h = \dot{m}_h c_{ph} =$ Heat capacity or water equivalent of hot fluid and kJ/sec.k

$\qquad C_c = \dot{m}_c c_{pc} =$ Heat capacity or water equivalent of cold fluid; kJ/sec.k

$\dot{m}_h$ and $\dot{m}_c$ are the mass flow rates of fluids and C_{ph} and C_{pc} are the respective specific heats.

$$\therefore dt_h - dt_c = -dQ\left[\frac{1}{C_h} + \frac{1}{C_c}\right]$$

$$\text{So,} \quad d\theta = -dQ\left[\frac{1}{C_h} + \frac{1}{C_c}\right] \qquad \ldots(6)$$

Substituting the value of dQ from equation (5), the above equation becomes

$$d\theta = -U \cdot dA\left(t_h - t_c\right)\left[\frac{1}{C_h} + \frac{1}{C_c}\right]$$

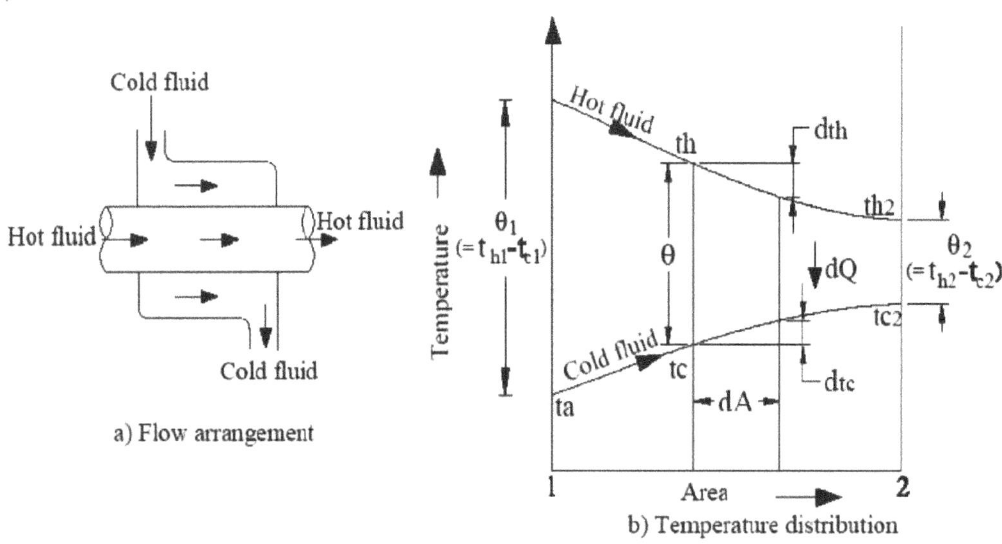

Figure 12 : Parallel flow heat exchanger

$$\therefore d\theta = -U \cdot dA \cdot \theta \left[\frac{1}{C_h} + \frac{1}{C_c} \right]$$

$$\therefore \frac{d\theta}{\theta} = -U \cdot dA \left[\frac{1}{C_h} + \frac{1}{C_c} \right]$$

Integrating between inlet and outlet conditions (i.e. from $A = 0$ to $A = A$), we get

$$\int_1^2 \frac{d\theta}{\theta} = -\left[\frac{1}{C_h} + \frac{1}{C_c} \right] \int_{A=0}^{A=A} U \cdot dA$$

$$\therefore \ln(\theta_2 / \theta_1) = -UA \left[\frac{1}{C_h} + \frac{1}{C_c} \right] \qquad \qquad ...(7)$$

Total heat transfer rate between the two fluids is given by,

$$Q = C_h \left(t_{h1} - t_{h2} \right) = C_c \left(t_{c2} - t_{c1} \right) \qquad \qquad ...(8)$$

So, $\dfrac{1}{C_h} = \dfrac{t_{h1} - t_{h2}}{Q}$

and $\dfrac{1}{C_c} = \dfrac{t_{c2} - t_{c1}}{Q}$

Substituting the values of $\dfrac{1}{C_h}$ and $\dfrac{1}{C_c}$ into equation (7), we have

$$\ln(\theta_2 / \theta_1) = -UA \left[\frac{t_{h1} - t_{h2}}{Q} + \frac{t_{c2} - t_{c1}}{Q} \right]$$

$$= \frac{UA}{Q} \left(t_{h2} - t_{c2} \right) - \left(t_{h1} - t_{c1} \right) = \frac{UA}{Q} \left(\theta_2 - \theta_1 \right)$$

$$\therefore Q = \frac{UA \left(\theta_2 - \theta_1 \right)}{\ln(\theta_2 / \theta_1)}$$

Now, $Q = U A \theta_m$

where, $\Delta t_m = \theta_m = \dfrac{\theta_2 - \theta_1}{\ln(\theta_2 / \theta_1)} = \dfrac{\theta_1 - \theta_2}{\ln(\theta_1 / \theta_2)}$

Q.2 A) "Generally, fin is provided to increase the heat transfer rate but by providing fin heat transfer may decrease." Justify the statement in context to heat transfer.

Fins are extended surfaces used to enhance the rate of heat transfer between a solid surface and the surrounding fluid by increasing the effective surface area. The basic principle relies on Fourier's law of heat conduction and Newton's law of cooling, which suggest that a greater surface area facilitates higher heat transfer, provided all other factors remain constant.

However, the effectiveness of a fin depends on several parameters including thermal conductivity of the material, geometry, and the convective heat transfer coefficient of the surrounding fluid. In certain cases, instead of increasing heat transfer, the addition of fins may lead to a decrease in heat dissipation. This occurs when:

1. Low Thermal Conductivity of Fin Material: If the material used for the fin has low thermal conductivity (e.g., plastic or wood), the temperature gradient along the fin length becomes minimal, and the heat conducted to the fin tip is negligible. In such cases, the fin acts more like an insulator than a conductor, impeding rather than aiding heat transfer.

2. Poor Convective Conditions: If the surrounding fluid has a very low convective heat transfer coefficient (such as still air), the additional surface area provided by the fin may not be utilized efficiently. As a result, the fin's contribution to heat transfer may be minimal or even counterproductive.

3. Excessive Fin Size or Number: Adding too many fins or using excessively large fins can lead to flow obstruction or increased thermal resistance at the fin base. This can reduce the effectiveness of heat transfer from the primary surface.

4. Fin Efficiency and Effectiveness: A fin's efficiency (η) is defined as the ratio of actual heat transfer from the fin to the ideal heat transfer if the entire fin were at the base temperature. When efficiency is low, the fin contributes little to overall heat transfer. If fin effectiveness (ε), defined as the ratio of heat transfer with the fin to that without the fin, is less than 1, the fin actually reduces heat transfer.

B   a) **Explain the situation when the addition of fins to a surface is not useful.**
    b) **Under what situations does the fin efficiency becomes 100%.**

a) The addition of fins to a surface is intended to increase the rate of heat transfer by enlarging the effective surface area in contact with the surrounding fluid. However, in certain situations, the addition of fins does not result in any significant improvement and may even hinder heat transfer. These situations include:

1. Low Thermal Conductivity of Fin Material: If the material used to manufacture the fin has low thermal conductivity (e.g., plastic, wood), it cannot effectively transfer heat along its length. As a result, the temperature drop along the fin is too small to drive meaningful heat exchange, making the fin ineffective.

2. High Convective Heat Transfer Coefficient (h): When the surface is already exposed to a high convective heat transfer coefficient (e.g., forced convection in liquids or gases), the benefit of increasing surface area becomes marginal. In such cases, the original surface is already efficient in transferring heat, and adding fins provides little to no gain.

3. Short Fin Length or Very Thin Fins: Short or thin fins may not offer enough additional surface area to significantly influence the overall heat transfer. The cost and complexity of adding them may outweigh the minimal gain achieved.

4. Low Temperature Difference: If the temperature difference between the fin surface and the surrounding fluid is small, the driving force for heat transfer is weak. In such conditions, even with increased surface area, the rate of heat transfer remains low.
5. Space and Flow Interference: In compact systems or devices, the addition of fins might obstruct airflow or fluid flow, increasing resistance and reducing effective heat transfer. This is especially problematic in electronics cooling, where space is a critical factor.
6. Fin Effectiveness Less than Unity ($\varepsilon < 1$): The effectiveness of a fin is defined as the ratio of the heat transfer with the fin to the heat transfer without the fin. If this value is less than one, it implies that the fin is actually decreasing the overall heat dissipation.

In summary, fins are not useful when the material, geometry, or operating conditions prevent effective heat conduction through the fin or efficient heat convection from the fin surface to the surroundings.

b) Fin efficiency becomes 100% ($\eta = 1$) when the entire fin remains at the same temperature as the base throughout its length. This ideal condition implies that there is no temperature drop along the fin, and every part of the fin is contributing equally and maximally to the heat transfer process.

This scenario can occur under the following conditions:
1. Infinitely High Thermal Conductivity of Fin Material:
    o If the fin material has extremely high thermal conductivity (e.g., idealized case or materials like pure copper or silver), it can instantly conduct heat across its entire length, keeping the temperature uniform.
2. Very Short Fin Length:
    o When the fin is extremely short, the temperature gradient along the fin becomes negligible. As a result, the entire fin remains nearly at the base temperature.
3. Extremely High Convective Heat Transfer Coefficient (h):
    o If the surrounding fluid has a very high convective heat transfer coefficient, heat is rapidly removed from all parts of the fin, minimizing the temperature difference between the base and the tip.
4. Infinitesimally Thin Fin:
    o In theory, if the fin is extremely thin, the conduction resistance along the fin becomes negligible, and the temperature remains almost constant throughout.

While achieving 100% efficiency is practically impossible due to inevitable temperature drops along the length of the fin, these are the theoretical conditions under which it could occur. In real-world applications, efficiency is always less than 1 but can approach high values with optimal design.

C   **Write the most general equation in Cartesian coordinates for heat transfer by conduction. Hence, deduce the above equation for the following cases with suitable assumptions; (i) Laplace equation, (ii) Poisson equation, and (iii) Fourier equation.**

The general equation for heat transfer by conduction in a three-dimensional, isotropic medium with internal heat generation is given by the **heat conduction equation** (also known as the energy equation). In Cartesian coordinates (x, y, z), it is expressed as:

$$\frac{\partial}{\partial x}\left(k\frac{\partial T}{\partial x}\right) + \frac{\partial}{\partial y}\left(k\frac{\partial T}{\partial y}\right) + \frac{\partial}{\partial z}\left(k\frac{\partial T}{\partial z}\right) + \dot{q} = \rho c_p \frac{\partial T}{\partial t}$$

(i) Laplace Equation

Assumptions:

- Steady-state heat conduction $\left(\frac{\partial T}{\partial t} = 0\right)$

- No internal heat generation $(\dot{q} = 0)$
  - Constant thermal conductivity k

Equation reduces to:

$$k\left(\frac{\partial^2 T}{\partial x^2} + \frac{\partial^2 T}{\partial y^2} + \frac{\partial^2 T}{\partial z^2}\right) = 0$$

Dividing by k (since $k \neq 0$):

$$\frac{\partial^2 T}{\partial x^2} + \frac{\partial^2 T}{\partial y^2} + \frac{\partial^2 T}{\partial z^2} = 0$$

This is known as the **Laplace Equation**.

(ii) Poisson Equation

Assumptions:

- Steady-state heat conduction $\left(\frac{\partial T}{\partial t} = 0\right)$

- Internal heat generation exists $(\dot{q} \neq 0)$

- Constant thermal conductivity k

Equation reduces to:

$$k\left(\frac{\partial^2 T}{\partial x^2} + \frac{\partial^2 T}{\partial y^2} + \frac{\partial^2 T}{\partial z^2}\right) + \dot{q} = 0$$

Dividing by k:

$$\frac{\partial^2 T}{\partial x^2} + \frac{\partial^2 T}{\partial y^2} + \frac{\partial^2 T}{\partial z^2} = -\frac{\dot{q}}{k}$$

This is known as the **Poisson Equation**.

(iii) Fourier Equation

Assumptions:

- Transient (unsteady) heat conduction $\left(\frac{\partial T}{\partial t} \neq 0\right)$

- No internal heat generation $(\dot{q} = 0)$

- Constant thermal conductivity k

Equation becomes:

$$k \left(\frac{\partial^2 T}{\partial x^2} + \frac{\partial^2 T}{\partial y^2} + \frac{\partial^2 T}{\partial z^2} \right) = \rho c_p \frac{\partial T}{\partial t}$$

Dividing by ρc_p:

$$\frac{\partial T}{\partial t} = \alpha \left(\frac{\partial^2 T}{\partial x^2} + \frac{\partial^2 T}{\partial y^2} + \frac{\partial^2 T}{\partial z^2} \right)$$

Where $\alpha = \frac{k}{\rho c_p}$ is the **thermal diffusivity**.

This is known as the **Fourier Equation** or the **heat diffusion equation**.

OR

C   **A steel fin (k=55W/mK) with a cross-section of an equilateral triangle, 5mm on the side is 80mm long. It is attached to a plane wall maintained at 350⁰C. The ambient air temperature is 40⁰C and unit surface conductance is 100W/m²K. Calculate the heat dissipation rate by assuming the fin as a rod with the tip of the fin is insulated.**

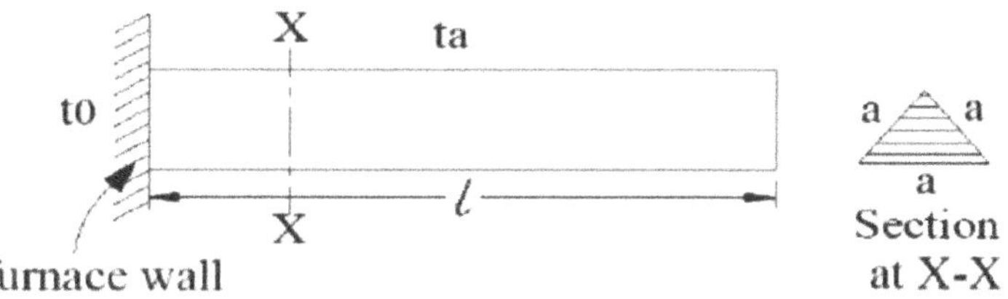

Figure

Heat dissipated by the rod. Q:

The heat flow from the rod (considering tip of the fin to be insulated) is given by,

$$Q = k \cdot A_{cs} \cdot m \left(t_o - t_a \right) \tanh \left(mL \right)$$

$$m = \sqrt{\frac{p \cdot h}{A_{cs} \cdot k}} \;:\; p = 3a \,, \; A_{cs} = \frac{1}{2} a \left(\frac{\sqrt{3}}{2} a \right) = \frac{\sqrt{3}}{2} a^2$$

$$= \sqrt{\frac{3a \times 90}{\frac{\sqrt{3}}{4} a^2 \times 54}} = 48.06\, m^{-1}$$

$$\therefore Q = 54 \times \left(\frac{\sqrt{3}}{4} (0.005)^2 \right) \times 48.06 \times (400 - 50) \tanh (48.06 \times 0.082)$$

$$= \mathbf{9.82\ W}$$

Q.3 A) What is critical radius of insulation? Explain its importance in electrical and thermal system.

The critical radius of insulation is a specific value of insulation thickness at which the heat transfer from a cylindrical or spherical object is maximized. Unlike flat surfaces, where adding insulation always reduces heat transfer, in cylindrical and spherical systems (like wires or pipes), adding insulation initially increases heat loss up to a certain point—the critical radius—after which further addition of insulation decreases heat loss.

Importance in Thermal Systems:

1. Heat Loss Management: In thermal systems such as steam pipes or hot water lines, applying insulation reduces heat loss. However, if the insulation thickness is below the critical radius, heat loss may increase due to increased outer surface area exposed to convection. Knowing the critical radius helps in designing efficient insulation that actually reduces heat loss.
2. Efficient Design: Understanding the critical radius allows engineers to determine the minimum effective insulation thickness needed. Adding insulation beyond this point ensures that heat loss is minimized without unnecessary material costs.
3. Avoiding Overheating: In systems where excessive insulation might trap heat, such as in electronics or electrical systems, identifying the critical radius prevents unintentional heat build-up that could damage components.

Importance in Electrical Systems:

1. Insulated Electrical Wires: Electrical wires generate heat due to resistance. When insulation is added, if its thickness is below the critical radius, the outer surface area increases, which can improve heat dissipation initially. However, exceeding the critical radius begins to trap heat, potentially leading to overheating and failure.
2. Thermal Safety of Devices: Devices like transformers, electric motors, and batteries rely on thermal insulation for safety. Proper understanding of the critical radius ensures that insulation materials do not compromise heat dissipation.

B **Compare the value of effectiveness for the counter and parallel flow for regenerator for NTU = 2.5.**

In heat exchanger analysis, effectiveness (ε) is a measure of how effectively a heat exchanger transfers heat relative to the maximum possible heat transfer. It depends on the type of flow arrangement and the Number of Transfer Units (NTU).

1. Counterflow Heat Exchanger (balanced flow, $C_r = 1$)

$$\varepsilon_{\text{counter}} = \frac{NTU}{1 + NTU} = \frac{2.5}{1 + 2.5} = \frac{2.5}{3.5} \approx 0.714$$

2. Parallel Flow Heat Exchanger (balanced flow, $C_r = 1$)

$$\varepsilon_{\text{parallel}} = \frac{1 - e^{-2 \cdot NTU}}{1 + C_r} = \frac{1 - e^{-5}}{2}$$

$$e^{-5} \approx 0.0067 \Rightarrow \varepsilon_{\text{parallel}} \approx \frac{1 - 0.0067}{2} = \frac{0.9933}{2} \approx 0.4966$$

At NTU = 2.5, the counterflow regenerator has significantly higher effectiveness ($\sim71.4\%$) than the parallel flow regenerator ($\sim49.7\%$).

This demonstrates that counterflow configurations are more thermally efficient, especially at higher NTU values, and are therefore preferred in regenerative heat exchanger designs.

C **Explain with neat sketch, the various regimes in boiling and explain the condition for the growth of bubbles. What is the effect of bubble size on boiling?**

To conduct an experiment on boiling, platinum wire is inserted in pool of water. An electric supply is given to wire to increase its temperature.

In case of pool boiling or forced convection boiling, the six different region occurs with increase in heat flux. The different regions of boiling are shown in figure 1, where heat flux q is plotted with respect to excess temperature (Δte).

Free convection boiling (Region I): -
In the region I, the liquid near the wire gets slightly superheated and this superheated liquid moves slowly at the liquid - vapour interface due to density difference, where evaporation of liquid takes place. This region occures where $\Delta te \leq 5^0C$ (up to point A). This process is shown in fig.2 (a).

Nucleate boiling (Region II and III) :- The nucleate boiling occurs in range of Δte as $5^0C \leq \Delta te \leq 30^0C$. (From point A to point C).

This region may be divided in two regions (A-B) and (B-C). In region II (A-B), the bubbles start forming at some nucleation sites on surface of wire. These bubbles will condensein liquid after deattachment. This process is shown in fig. 2(b). and fig 2(c). This region is called as unstable nucleate boiling. As the excess temperature further increases, the number of nucleation sites increases and thus bubble growth increases. This region III (B-C) is called as stable nucleate boiling. The bubble formed also gets combined and form slugs, as shown in fig.2(d). The nucleate boiling is a process in which maximum amount of heat is transferred. As seen from the fig.1 that q increases with increase in Δte, and reaches the maximum point C. This maximum value is also called as critical heat flux. As shown in figure 1, there is a point P between points A and C, where heat transfer co-efficient is maximum. Between points P and C, heat transfer co-efficient decreases but q increases due to very large increase in Δte. So as far as possible all boiling equipments should be run in region A-C and nearer to point P.

Transition Boiling (Region IV):-
With further increase in Δte, the formation of bubbles is so large that some bubble combine and form partial film on heating surface. This film offers thermal ressitance to heat flow and thus heat flux q decreases. This region (C-D) occures in a range of around $30^0C \leq \Delta te \leq 120^0C$. It is also called as unstable film boiling. This process is shown in fig.2 (e).

Film boiling (Region V and VI) :-
This region starts at point D, where film has completely covered the entire heating surface (fig 2 (f)) and the heat flux is minimum. This point is called as Leiden frost point. After that with increase in Δte (above 120^0C) the heat transfer due to conduction through film takes place. It is also called as a stable film boiling. With further increase in Δte, the heating surface becomes bright and thermal radiation from the surface becomes dominant.

Critical heat flux (Burn out point):-
The point C on the curve in fig.1, where the maximum heat flux is reached. It occurs at around $\Delta te \leq 35^0 C$. After this point, q starts to decrease. This heat flux is called as critical heat flux qcr and Δte is called as critical excess temperature $\Delta te,cr$. At this point, the temeprature may exceed the melting point of wire, thus it is also called a burn out point.

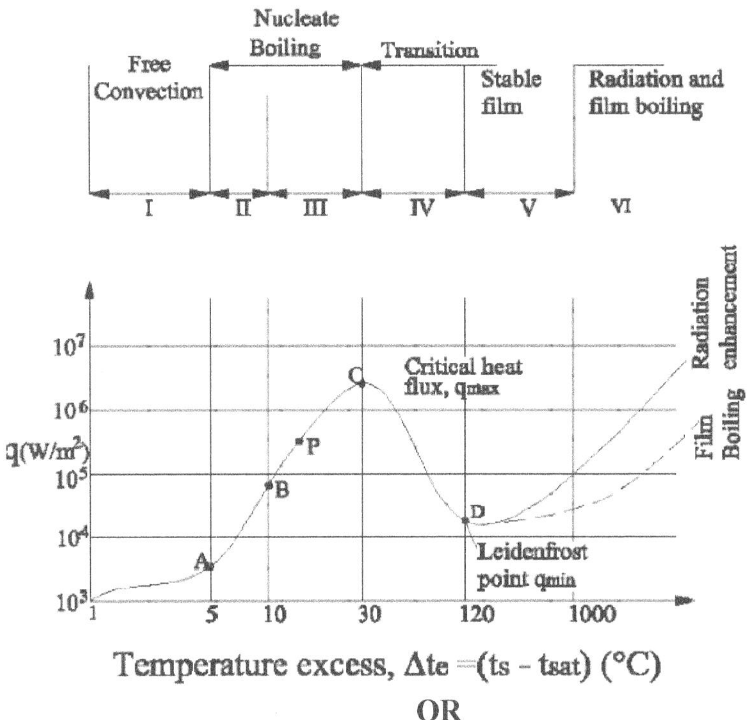

Temperature excess, $\Delta te = (ts - tsat)$ (°C)

OR

Q.3 A) Write three properties of shape factor.

Three properties of shape factor are:
1. Dimensionless Quantity: Shape factor is a ratio and has no units. It provides a comparative measure of how a shape deviates from an ideal or reference form (like a circle or square).
2. Geometry-Dependent: Shape factor depends solely on the geometry of the object, not its size. This means two shapes of the same form but different scales will have the same shape factor.
3. Used to Characterize Efficiency or Performance: In various fields (like heat transfer, structural mechanics, or image analysis), shape factor helps evaluate performance characteristics. For example, in heat transfer, it helps assess thermal efficiency; in structural analysis, it influences strength calculations.

B   Write the general differential equation in Cartesian coordinates for 3D unsteady heat conduction by considering an infinitesimal volume element. Deduce there from the conduction equations for the following cases;
(i) Steady-state 1-D flow with heat generation at a uniform rate within the material.

$$\frac{\partial}{\partial x}\left(k_x\frac{\partial t}{\partial x}\right)+\frac{\partial}{\partial y}\left(k_y\frac{\partial t}{\partial y}\right)+\frac{\partial}{\partial z}\left(k_z\frac{\partial t}{\partial z}\right)+\dot{q}_g = \rho.c.\frac{\partial t}{\partial \tau}$$

or, using the **vector operator** ∇, we get

$$\nabla.(k\nabla t)+\dot{q}_g = \rho.c.\frac{\partial t}{\partial \tau}$$

This is known as the general heat conduction equation for 'non-homogeneous anisotropic material', 'Self heat generating' and 'unsteady three-dimensional heat flow.'

Case (iii) Steady state and one-dimensional heat transer :

$$\frac{\partial^2 t}{\partial x^2}+\frac{\dot{q}_g}{k}=0$$

C **State the relationship between Nusselt number, Grashoff number and Prandtl number in case of heat transfer by nature convection from a vertical plate.**

Solution : Here in case of free convection velocity V, which was responsible for flow in forced convection is replaced by variables β, g, Δt, because here the velocity of fluid is very slow and flow is caused due to density difference. Combined $(\beta g \Delta t)$ represents buoyancy parameter which is causing the flow, so we will consider it as a single quantity.

Considering M-L-T-θ-H system here. The dimensions of various quantities are :

Variable	Symbol	Dimension
Heat Transfer co-efficient	h	$HL^{-2}T^{-1}\theta^{-1}$
Co-efficient of thermal expansion	β	θ^{-1}
Gravitational Acceleration	g	LT^{-2}
Temperature Difference	ΔT	θ
Characteristic length	l	L
Fluid density	ρ	ML^{-3}
Fluid viscosity	μ	$ML^{-1}T^{-1}$
Fluid Thermal conductivity	k	$HL^{-1}T^{-1}\theta^{-1}$
Specific heat (heat capacity)	C_p	$HM^{-1}\theta^{-1}$

or $\quad f'\left(h, \mu, \rho, k, C_p, \beta g \Delta t, l\right) = 0$

If we consider $(\beta g \Delta t)$ as combined quantity total quantities involved will be seven & no. of fundamental quantities used here as five. So no. of non-dimensional π group will be $(7-5) = 2$ only, which will not satisfy the required answer. (i.e. $Nu = \phi\left(Gr, Pr\right)$). Thus, we need to consider (βg) and (Δt) are two separate quantities for some cases. So now total quantities will be eight so $(\beta g \Delta t)$ & thus no. of π-groups will be 3.

But in this case, no. of repeated variables will be 4, because, no flow property (V or g) is there. Selecting l (geometric), μ (fluid property), $\beta g \Delta t$ (temp. property), k (thermal property) as repeatating quantities, we get π_1-term.

$$\pi_1 = \mu^{a_1} k^{b_1} \left(\beta g \Delta t\right)^{c_1} (l)^{d_1} h \qquad \qquad ...(I)$$

Putting dimensions for all, we get

$$M^o L^o T^o \theta^o H^o = \left[ML^{-1}T^{-1}\right]^{a_1} \left[HL^{-1}T^{-1}\theta^{-1}\right]^{b_1} \left[LT^{-2}\right]^{c_1} \left[L\right]^{d_1} \left[HL^{-2}T^{-1}\theta^{-1}\right]$$

Equating components for M, L, T, θ & H :

For M : $\quad 0 \quad = a_1$

$\quad$ L : $\quad 0 \quad = -a_1 - b_1 + c_1 + d_1 - 2$

$\quad$ T : $\quad 0 \quad = -a_1 - b_1 - 2c_1 - 1$

$\quad$ θ : $\quad 0 \quad = -b_1 - 1$

$\quad$ H : $\quad 0 \quad = b_1 + 1$

Equating above equations we get

$$a_1 = 0, \ b_1 = -1, \ c_1 = 0, \ d_1 = 1$$

Putting these values in equation (I)

$$\pi_1 = \frac{hl}{k}$$

π_2-**term** : $\pi_2 = \mu^{a_2} k^{b_2} \left(\beta g \Delta t\right)^{c_2} l^{d_2} \rho$

By doing same procedure we will get $\pi_2 = \dfrac{l^3 \rho^2 \left(\beta g \Delta t\right)}{\mu^2}$

π_3-**term** : $\pi_3 = \mu^{a_3} k^{b_3} \left(\beta g \Delta t\right)^{c_3} l^{d_3} C_p$

We will get $\pi_3 = \dfrac{\mu C_p}{k}$

Now, $\pi_1 = \phi\left(\pi_2, \pi_3\right)$

$$\therefore \frac{hl}{k} = \phi\left(\frac{l^3 \rho^2 \left(\beta g \Delta t\right)}{\mu^2} \cdot \frac{\mu C_p}{k}\right)$$

Thus, $Nu = \phi\left(Gr, Pr\right)$

or $\qquad Nu = C_1 Gr^{c_2} Pr^{c_3}$

where c_1, c_2, c_3 constants are found out by experiments.

Q.4 **A) Justify the use of polished surfaces in thermal insulation systems from the perspective of radiation.**

Polished surfaces are used in thermal insulation systems to minimize heat transfer by thermal radiation. Because of:

1. Low Emissivity of Polished Surfaces
   - Polished (shiny or reflective) surfaces have low emissivity, meaning they emit very little thermal radiation.
   - Emissivity is a measure of a surface's ability to emit infrared energy. A perfectly polished metal surface (like aluminum) may have an emissivity as low as 0.03–0.05, while a black, rough surface may have emissivity close to 1.0.
   - Lower emissivity means less radiative heat loss from the surface.

2. Reduced Absorption of Radiation
   - Polished surfaces also reflect most of the incoming radiation rather than absorbing it.
   - This reflection reduces the amount of thermal radiation absorbed from the surroundings, thereby lowering heat gain in systems meant to stay cool.

3. Improved Thermal Performance
   - In high-temperature insulation systems (like in vacuum flasks, spacecraft, or cryogenic containers), radiation can be a significant mode of heat transfer.
   - Using multiple layers of polished reflective surfaces (e.g., multilayer insulation) can drastically reduce radiative heat transfer, enhancing the overall thermal insulation performance.

Hence, polished surfaces reduce radiative heat transfer by minimizing both emission and absorption of thermal radiation, making them highly effective for thermal insulation in environments where radiation is a dominant heat transfer mode.

B **Define Biot number and Fourier number, and point out their physical significance.**

The Biot number is a dimensionless quantity defined as:

Bi=hLc/ k.

Physical Significance:
   - The Biot number compares internal thermal resistance (conduction) within a body to external thermal resistance (convection) across the surface.

- Bi << 1: Conduction inside the object is much faster than convection at the surface → temperature inside the body is nearly uniform (lumped system assumption is valid).
- Bi > 1: There are significant temperature gradients within the object → internal conduction limits heat transfer.

The Fourier number is a dimensionless time parameter defined as: $Fo = \alpha t / L^2$

Physical Significance:

- The Fourier number indicates how much heat has diffused through a material over time.
- Higher Fo means more heat penetration and faster temperature equalization.
- In transient heat conduction, it helps determine how quickly the temperature changes inside a body.

C   **Define radiation shield. Prove that if radiation shields of the emissivity same as the emissivity of one parallel plate is inserted between two parallel plates net heat transfer rate due to radiation is reduced to half as compared to without shield.**

Radiation heat transfer between two surfaces may be reduced either by using the materials which are highly reflective (very low emissivity) or by placing a thin shield (radiation shields) between them.

The radiation shields increase the thermal resistance in the path of radiation heat transfer and hence reduce the heat flow rate without actually removing any heat from the overall system. A very effective insulation is provided by using many layers of radiation shields separated by a vacuum.

Thin sheets of plastic coated with highly reflecting metallic films on both sides serves as very effective radiation shields. They are used in cryogenic and space applications like insulation of liquid oxygen or nitrogen tanks.

Refer figure no.18. Let us consider two parallel plates 1 and 2 having areas $A1 = A2 = A$ at temperature T1 and T2 respectively.

For the radiation heat exchange between two plates,

$$(Q_{12})_{net} = \frac{A\sigma\left(T_1^4 - T_2^4\right)}{\dfrac{1}{\epsilon_1} + \dfrac{1}{\epsilon_2} - 1} \qquad \ldots(46)$$

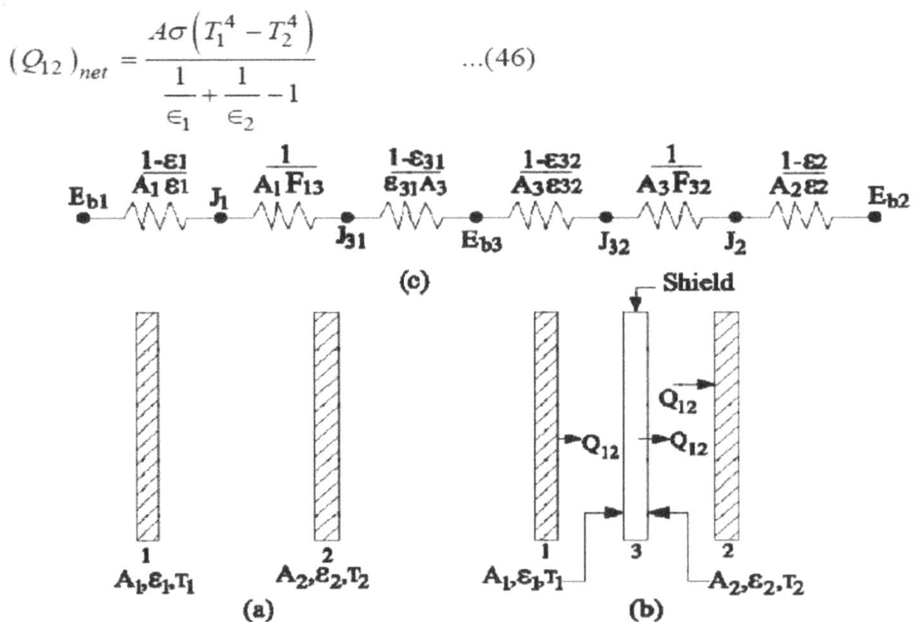

Fig. 18 : Radiation shield placed between two large parallel plates and radiation shield.

Refer figure no. 18 (b). Radiation shield with area A_3 and temperature T_3 is placed between two plates. So the heat exchange takes place between 1,3 and 3,2.

$$\therefore \left(Q_{13}\right)_{net} = \frac{A.\sigma\left(T_1^4 - T_3^4\right)}{\dfrac{1}{\epsilon_1} + \dfrac{1}{\epsilon_3} - 1} \qquad ...(47)$$

$$and \ \left(Q_{32}\right)_{net} = \frac{A.\sigma\left(T_3^4 - T_2^4\right)}{\dfrac{1}{\epsilon_3} + \dfrac{1}{\epsilon_2} - 1} \qquad ...(48)$$

Since the radiation shield does not remove or deliver heat from the system, $\left(Q_{13}\right)_{net} = \left(Q_{32}\right)_{net}$.

$$\therefore \frac{A.\sigma\left(T_1^4 - T_3^4\right)}{\dfrac{1}{\epsilon_1} + \dfrac{1}{\epsilon_3} - 1} = \frac{A.\sigma\left(T_3^4 - T_2^4\right)}{\dfrac{1}{\epsilon_3} + \dfrac{1}{\epsilon_2} - 1} \qquad ...(49)$$

$$So. \ T_3^4 = \frac{T_1^4\left(\dfrac{1}{\epsilon_2} + \dfrac{1}{\epsilon_3} - 1\right) + T_2^4\left(\dfrac{1}{\epsilon_1} + \dfrac{1}{\epsilon_3} - 1\right)}{\left(\dfrac{1}{\epsilon_2} + \dfrac{1}{\epsilon_3} - 1\right) + \left(\dfrac{1}{\epsilon_1} + \dfrac{1}{\epsilon_3} - 1\right)} \qquad ...(50)$$

By replacing the value of T_3 in equation (49) using equation (50) and simplyfying.

$$\therefore \left(Q_{12}\right)_{net} = \frac{A.\sigma\left(T_1^4 - T_3^4\right)}{\left(\dfrac{1}{\epsilon_1} + \dfrac{1}{\epsilon_3} - 1\right) + \left(\dfrac{1}{\epsilon_2} + \dfrac{1}{\epsilon_3} - 1\right)} \qquad ...(51)$$

Now, dividing equation (51) by equation (46), we have

$$\therefore \frac{\left[\left(Q_{12}\right)_{net}\right] with \ shield}{\left[\left(Q_{12}\right)_{net}\right] without \ shield} = \frac{\left(\dfrac{1}{\epsilon_1} + \dfrac{1}{\epsilon_2} - 1\right)}{\left(\dfrac{1}{\epsilon_1} + \dfrac{1}{\epsilon_3} - 1\right) + \left(\dfrac{1}{\epsilon_2} + \dfrac{1}{\epsilon_3} - 1\right)} \qquad ...(52)$$

equation (52) is the most general equation for heat transfer by radiation with shield to without shield.

If $\epsilon_1 = \epsilon_3 = \epsilon_2 = \epsilon$, than above equation is reduced to,

$$\therefore \frac{\left[\left(Q_{12}\right)_{net}\right] with \ shield}{\left[\left(Q_{12}\right)_{net}\right] without \ shield} = \frac{(1+1-1)}{(1+1-1)+(1+1-1)} = \frac{1}{2}$$

OR

Q.4 **Differentiate mean film temperature and bulk mean temperature.**

The mean film temperature is the average temperature between the surface and the surrounding fluid. Used to evaluate fluid properties (like viscosity, thermal conductivity, etc.) when calculating heat transfer coefficients in convection.

The bulk mean temperature is the average temperature of the fluid flowing through a pipe or duct, weighted by mass flow rate or energy flow.

Used in calculating heat transfer between a flowing fluid and a surface, especially in forced convection.

Aspect	Mean Film Temperature (Tf)	Bulk Mean Temperature (Tm)
Used For	Evaluating fluid properties for calculations	Energy balance in flowing fluids
Based On	Surface and ambient temperatures	Cross-sectional average temperature of flowing fluid
Typical Application	Free and forced convection	Internal flows (pipes, ducts, channels)

B **What is lumped system analysis? What are the assumption made in the lumped system analysis and when it is applicable?**

Lumped system analysis is a simplification used in transient heat transfer where the temperature within a solid body is assumed to be uniform at any given time during the heating or cooling process. This method greatly simplifies the solution of the heat transfer problem by converting a partial differential equation into an ordinary differential equation.

Assumptions in Lumped System Analysis:

1. Uniform Temperature Distribution: The temperature inside the solid is spatially uniform (no internal temperature gradients).
2. Constant Material Properties: Thermal conductivity, density, and specific heat are assumed to be constant.
3. Negligible Radiation and Conduction Losses (Unless Considered): Only convection (typically) is considered for heat exchange with the environment.
4. Valid for Small Biot Number: The Biot number must be less than 0.1. This ensures that internal conduction is much faster than surface convection.

The analysis is valid when:

- Biot number <0.1
- The body is thermally small or made of high thermal conductivity material (like metals).
- The external heat transfer (usually convection) is relatively slow compared to internal conduction.

C **What is heat exchanger? Classify the heat exchanger types with example.**

Heat exchangers are devices used to transfer heat between two or more fluids at different temperatures. They are widely used in industries such as power generation, chemical processing, refrigeration, and HVAC systems. Heat exchangers can be broadly classified based on various criteria, as described below:

1. Based on the Nature of Heat Exchange Process:

- Direct Contact Heat Exchangers: In these heat exchangers, the two fluids come into direct physical contact and exchange heat.

They are typically used when mixing of fluids is permissible. Examples include cooling towers and jet condensers.

- Indirect Contact Heat Exchangers: In this type, the fluids do not mix and are separated by a solid wall. Heat is transferred through conduction and convection across the wall. These are the most common types in industrial applications.

2. Based on Relative Direction of Fluid Flow:

- Parallel Flow Heat Exchangers: Both the hot and cold fluids enter the exchanger at the same end and move in the same direction. This configuration is simple but less efficient in terms of temperature change.
- Counter Flow Heat Exchangers: The fluids enter the exchanger from opposite ends and flow in opposite directions. This arrangement provides the highest efficiency and greater temperature difference between fluids.
- Cross Flow Heat Exchangers: The two fluids flow perpendicular to each other. These are commonly used in air-cooled applications such as automobile radiators.

3. Based on Design and Construction:

- Shell and Tube Heat Exchangers: Composed of a series of tubes enclosed in a cylindrical shell. One fluid flow through the tubes, while the other flows outside the tubes within the shell. They are widely used in oil refineries and power plants.
- Plate Heat Exchangers: Made up of multiple thin metal plates with large surface areas, stacked together to form channels for fluid flow. They provide high heat transfer efficiency and are used in food processing and chemical industries.
- Finned Tube Heat Exchangers: Incorporate fins on the tubes to increase the surface area and improve heat transfer, especially in air-side heat transfer applications.
- Double Pipe Heat Exchangers: Consist of one pipe inside another, allowing one fluid to flow through the inner pipe and another fluid through the annular space between the pipes. Suitable for small-scale applications.

4. Based on Number of Fluids:

- Two-Fluid Heat Exchangers: Involve the exchange of heat between two fluids. This is the most common configuration.
- Multi-Fluid Heat Exchangers: Designed to handle more than two fluids, often used in complex systems such as combined cycle power plants or chemical reactors.

5. Based on Heat Transfer Mechanism:

- Single Phase Heat Exchangers: Both fluids remain in the same phase (either liquid or gas) throughout the heat exchange process. No phase change occurs.
- Two-Phase Heat Exchangers: At least one fluid undergoes a phase change, such as condensation or evaporation. These are used in boilers, condensers, and evaporators.

6. Based on Transfer Process Configuration:

- Recuperative Heat Exchangers: The fluids flow on either side of a solid heat transfer surface without mixing. Heat is transferred directly through the separating wall. Examples include shell and tube and plate heat exchangers.

Regenerative Heat Exchangers: A single medium, usually a matrix or a rotating wheel, alternately stores heat from the hot fluid and transfers it to the cold fluid. These are typically used in gas turbines and air preheaters.

Q.5 **A) What is the significance of thermal conductivity in material selection for heat exchangers and insulators? Discuss its role in optimizing heat transfer.**

Thermal conductivity is a fundamental property that plays a crucial role in determining the efficiency and effectiveness of materials used in heat exchangers and insulation systems. It dictates how well heat can be transferred through a material.

1. Heat Exchangers:

Role of Thermal Conductivity:

- Enhancing Heat Transfer: In heat exchangers, the goal is to efficiently transfer heat between two fluids (or between a fluid and a solid surface). Materials with high thermal conductivity (e.g., copper, aluminum) are used in heat exchangers because they allow heat to move quickly from one fluid to another, optimizing the heat transfer rate.
- Improved Efficiency: Materials with higher thermal conductivity reduce the thermal resistance between the fluid and the heat exchange surface, enabling better performance. For instance, in a tube-in-tube heat exchanger, the metal tube with high thermal conductivity facilitates rapid heat transfer between the two fluids.
- Minimizing Thermal Gradients: A material with high thermal conductivity will result in more uniform temperature distributions, which helps to maintain the desired operating temperature throughout the heat exchanger.

Example Materials:

- Copper (high conductivity) and aluminum are commonly used in heat exchangers due to their superior thermal conductivity. They enable quicker and more efficient heat exchange in systems like HVAC systems, car radiators, or industrial heat exchangers.

2. Insulators:

Role of Thermal Conductivity:

- Reducing Heat Transfer: In insulation systems, the goal is to minimize heat transfer between two areas with different temperatures. To achieve this, materials with low thermal conductivity are selected, such as fiberglass, mineral wool, or polystyrene foam.
- Increasing Thermal Resistance: Materials with low thermal conductivity prevent heat from passing through easily, thus maintaining the desired temperature in a system. This is essential for applications such as building insulation, pipes, or cryogenic storage where maintaining low or high temperatures is critical.
- Maintaining Energy Efficiency: In insulating systems for buildings, pipes, and industrial applications, low thermal conductivity materials help reduce the amount of energy lost or gained, improving energy efficiency and reducing costs.

Example Materials:

- Fiberglass, mineral wool, and expanded polystyrene (EPS) have low thermal conductivity, making them effective insulators in both cold and hot environments.

Optimizing Heat Transfer Based on Thermal Conductivity:

1. For Heat Exchangers:
    - When selecting materials for heat exchangers, maximize the thermal conductivity to ensure that the heat can move quickly between the two fluids or surfaces.

However, material cost, weight, and corrosion resistance must also be considered.
- o The heat exchanger design (e.g., surface area, fluid velocity) can also influence how much heat is transferred, but the material's thermal conductivity is a fundamental factor in its performance.
2. For Insulators:
- o When selecting materials for insulation, minimize the thermal conductivity to reduce the rate of heat transfer. In some cases, materials with low conductivity are paired with air gaps or reflective layers to further reduce heat transfer through conduction, convection, or radiation.
- o The thickness of the insulation material and the temperature difference across it also influence heat transfer, but a lower thermal conductivity material will perform better overall.

B **Why is it important to analyze heat conduction through composite walls in industrial applications? Explain in brief, how to calculate the overall heat transfer rate in such systems.**

Analysing heat conduction through composite walls is crucial in industrial applications for several reasons:
1. Energy Efficiency: Understanding heat transfer helps in optimizing insulation and minimizing energy losses, leading to lower operational costs in industrial processes, HVAC systems, and buildings.
2. Safety: In industries where, high temperatures are involved (e.g., chemical, manufacturing), controlling heat flow is essential for safety, preventing overheating, and ensuring equipment operates within safe temperature limits.
3. Material Selection: Composite walls often consist of layers with different materials (insulation, metal, concrete, etc.), each having different thermal conductivities. Analysing heat transfer helps in selecting appropriate materials for specific temperature ranges and environmental conditions.
4. Regulatory Compliance: Many industries are required to comply with thermal performance standards. analysing heat conduction ensures that these regulations are met.

Calculating the Overall Heat Transfer Rate;
To calculate the overall heat transfer rate (Q) through a composite wall system, you typically treat each layer as a thermal resistance in series. The formula is:

$$Q = \Delta T / R_{total}$$

For a wall with multiple layers, the total resistance is the sum of the individual resistances:
$$R_{total} = R_1 + R_2 + \cdots + R_n$$

C **An egg with mean diameter of 4 cm and initially at 20°C is placed in a boiling water pan for 4 minutes and found to be boiled to the consumer's test. For how long should a similar egg for same consumer be boiled when taken from a refrigerator at 5°C. Take following properties for egg :**
$k = 10 \text{W} / \text{m}^0\text{C}$, $\rho = 1200 \text{kg} / \text{m}^3$, $C = 2 \text{kJ} / \text{kg}^0\text{C}$, $h = 100 \text{W} / \text{m}^{2\,0}\text{C}$

Given data : $\quad R = \dfrac{40}{2} = 20mm = 0.02m,\quad t_i = 20°C,\quad \tau = 60 \times 4 = 240\,sec.$

$k = 10\,W/m°C,\quad \rho = 1200\,kg/m^3,\quad c = 2000\,J/kg°C,\quad h = 100\,W/m^2 \cdot C$

For using the lump theory, the ref. condition is $Bi < 0.1$

$$Bi = \frac{h \cdot L_c}{k}$$

where, $L_c = \dfrac{v}{A_s} = \dfrac{\frac{4}{3}\pi R^3}{4\pi R^2} = \dfrac{R}{3}$

$$Bi = \frac{100 \times 0.02}{10 \times 3} = 0.067 < 0.1$$

we can use hemp theory.

a) The temperature variation with time is given by

$$\frac{t - t_a}{t_i - t_a} = e^{-\frac{hA_\rho}{\rho vc}\tau}$$

$$\frac{h \cdot As}{\rho vc} = \left(\frac{h}{\rho C}\right)\left(\frac{As}{V}\right) = \left(\frac{100}{1200 \times 2000}\right)\left(\frac{3}{0.02}\right) = 0.00625$$

$$\therefore \frac{t - 100}{20 - 100} = e^{-0.0025 \times 240} = 0.223$$

$$\therefore t = 100 + (20 - 100) \times 0.223 = 82.16°C$$

b) Now, let us find 'τ' when the given data is :

$$t_i = 5°C,\quad t_a = 100°C\ \&\ t = 82°C$$

$$\therefore \frac{82 - 100}{5 - 100} = e^{-0.00625\tau} = \frac{1}{e^{0.00625\tau}}$$

$$\therefore 0.1895 = \frac{1}{e^{0.00625\tau}}$$

$$\therefore e^{0.00625\tau} = \frac{1}{0.1895} = 5.277$$

$$\therefore 0.00625\tau = \ln 5.277 = 1.6633$$

$$\therefore \tau = \frac{1.6633}{0.00625} = 266.13\,sec$$

$$\tau = \mathbf{4.435min}$$

OR

Q.5 **A) What is the relevance of one-dimensional heat conduction analysis in practical applications? Explain with the example of heat transfer through a plane wall or cylinder.**

One-dimensional heat conduction analysis is a fundamental concept in thermodynamics and heat transfer that is commonly used to solve real-world problems where heat transfer occurs primarily in one direction. This simplification is especially useful when the temperature gradients in other directions are either negligible or relatively small. It provides an efficient way to predict how heat moves through materials in various practical applications, such as in insulation design, electronic devices, and construction.

Practical Applications;

1. Insulation Design: In buildings and HVAC systems, we often need to control heat transfer through walls, roofs, and floors to maintain energy efficiency. Using one-dimensional heat conduction analysis, we can determine the heat loss or gain through a plane wall or cylinder and design the correct thickness of insulation material to minimize energy consumption.

2. Electronics: For electronic devices, heat dissipation is crucial. One-dimensional heat conduction is often used to model heat flow through components like microchips or heat sinks, helping engineers design effective cooling systems.

3. Heat Exchangers: Heat exchangers transfer heat between fluids. In many cases, the heat conduction in the material walls between the fluids is analysed in one dimension (assuming that heat conduction across the wall thickness dominates the process).

4. Furnaces, Boilers, and Industrial Equipment: In industries that require the transfer of heat (like furnaces or boilers), one-dimensional heat conduction helps to design the walls and materials for optimal performance.

B **Discuss the principle behind why black surfaces absorb more radiant energy and how it enhances the efficiency of solar panels in converting sunlight to electricity.**

The key reason black surfaces absorb more radiant energy compared to other colors is related to light absorption and reflection. The color of a surface depends on the wavelengths of light it reflects, absorbs, and transmits.

☐ Black surfaces absorb more radiant energy because they reflect less light and absorb more wavelengths of sunlight, including those outside the visible spectrum (like infrared).

☐ In solar panels, increased absorption means more sunlight is converted into electrical energy, making the panels more efficient at generating electricity.

☐ By minimizing reflection losses, black surfaces help ensure that as much light as possible is absorbed by the solar cells.

☐ However, thermal management is important to prevent excessive heat buildup, which can reduce the efficiency of solar panels. Modern technologies address this challenge by using cooling techniques or specialized coatings.

C **A cylinder in vertical position is having dimension of 18 cm diameter and length 1.5 m is maintained at a temperature of 100^0C. It is kept in atmosphere having temperature 20^0C. Calculate the heat lost by cylinder surface to the atmosphere by free convection.**

Properties of air at mean film temperature 60^0C are as follows:

ρ=1.06kg/m³, υ=18.97*10⁻⁶m²/s, k=0.1042kJ/m.hr.⁰C, Cp=1.004kJ/kg⁰C.
Use the relation Nu=0.10(Gr.Pr)¹ᐟ³ (The symbols have their usual meanings)

Given data : $L = 1.5m,\ D = 18cm = 0.18m,\ t_s = 100°C,\ t_\infty = 20°C,\ \rho = 1.06 kg/m^3,$

$\upsilon = 18.97 \times 10^{-6} m^2/s,\ C_p = 1.004 kJ/kg°C = 1004 J/kg°C,$

$$k = 0.1042\,kJ/mh°C = \frac{0.1042 \times 10^3}{3600}\frac{W}{m°C} = 0.0289\,\frac{W}{m\,°C}$$

$$t_{mf} = \frac{t_s + t_\infty}{2} = \frac{100 + 20}{2} = 60°C$$

Here characteristic length L_c is Length L of the cylinder
Heat loss by free convection Q :

$$\mu = \rho\upsilon = 1.06 \times \left(18.97 \times 10^{-6} \times 3600\right) = 0.07239\,kg/mh$$

$$= \frac{0.07239}{3600} = 2 \times 10^{-5}\,\frac{kg}{m-s}$$

$$\beta = \frac{1}{T} = \frac{1}{273 + t_{mf}} = \frac{1}{273 + \left(\dfrac{100+20}{2}\right)} = 0.003\,K^{-1}$$

$$Gr = \frac{\beta g \Delta t L^3 \rho^2}{\mu^2} = \frac{L^3 g \beta \Delta t}{\upsilon^2}$$

$$= \frac{(1.5)^3 \times 9.81 \times 0.003 \times (100-20)}{\left(18.97 \times 10^{-6}\right)^2} = 2.208 \times 10^{10}$$

$$Pr = \frac{\mu C_p}{k} = \frac{2 \times 10^{-5} \times 1004}{0.0289} = 0.6948$$

$$Gr\,Pr = 2.208 \times 10^{10} \times 0.6948 = 1.54 \times 10^{10}$$

$$Nu = \frac{hL_c}{k} = 0.10\left(Gr\,Pr\right)^{\frac{1}{3}}$$

$$= 0.10\left(1.54 \times 10^{10}\right)^{\frac{1}{3}} = 248.79$$

$$\therefore\ h = \frac{248.79}{L} \times k$$

$$h = \frac{248.79 \times 0.0289}{1.5} = 4.793\,\frac{W}{m^2°C}$$

(Here Area is surface area of cylinder $= \pi DL$)

$\therefore$ Rate of heat loss, $Q = h \times$ Surface Area $\times \left(t_s - t_\infty\right),$

$$= 4.793 \times (\pi \times 0.18 \times 1.5)(100-20)$$

$$= \mathbf{325.27\ W}$$

PAPER 3_3151909: HEAT TRANSFER

SUMMER 2024 EXAM   DATE: 18/05/2024

Q.1 **Do as directed:**

A 1) **Define: Thermal diffusivity.**
2) **Arrange the material in descending order of their thermal conductivity; i) Water ii) Copper iii) Air and iv) Wood.**
3) **Define: Anisotropic material.**

1) Thermal diffusivity is a material-specific property that quantifies the rate at which heat diffuses through a substance. It is defined as the ratio of thermal conductivity to the product of density and specific heat capacity at constant pressure.

Thermal diffusivity indicates how quickly a material can respond to changes in temperature. A high thermal diffusivity means that the material conducts heat rapidly relative to its capacity to store thermal energy, resulting in a quick temperature adjustment. Conversely, materials with low thermal diffusivity are slow to respond to temperature changes, as they retain heat longer.

2) The materials listed can be arranged in descending order of their thermal conductivity as follows: Copper > Water > Wood > Air

3) An anisotropic material is a type of material whose physical or mechanical properties differ based on the direction in which they are measured. This directional dependency means that properties such as thermal conductivity, electrical conductivity, elasticity, or refractive index vary with orientation within the material structure.

B **Give four examples of free convection and four examples of forced convection observed from day-to-day life.**

Examples of Free Convection:

1. Heating of Air Around a Room Heater: Warm air rises naturally from the heater and is replaced by cooler air, creating a convection current without external force.
2. Boiling Water in a Pot: As water at the bottom is heated, it becomes less dense and rises, while cooler water moves downward, forming natural convection currents.
3. Cooling of Hot Beverage in a Cup: The hot liquid loses heat to the surrounding air, causing warmer air to rise and cooler air to move in, enabling free convection.
4. Air Circulation in a Refrigerator When the Door is Open: Warmer room air enters and rises while cooler, denser air descends, creating a natural convection cycle.

Examples of Forced Convection:

1. Blowing Air on Hot Food Using a Fan: The fan forces air movement over the food, enhancing the rate of heat transfer and cooling.
2. Water Circulation in a Car Radiator: A pump forces coolant to circulate through the engine and radiator, increasing heat removal by forced convection.
3. Airflow from an Air Conditioner: Fans inside the AC unit push cool air into the room, distributing it by forced convection.
4. Using a Hair Dryer: Heated air is blown across the hair using an electric fan, combining heat and forced air movement to dry hair efficiently.

C   **Explain the following with reference to a heat exchanger:**
    1. Fouling factor, Effectiveness of heat exchanger,
    2. Correction factor for multipass arrangement.

1. Fouling Factor

Fouling refers to the accumulation of unwanted materials such as scale, rust, biological growth, or chemical deposits on the heat transfer surfaces of a heat exchanger. This buildup creates an additional thermal resistance, reducing the overall heat transfer efficiency. The fouling factor (Rf) quantifies this resistance and is typically expressed in units of $(m^2 \cdot K)/W$.

The total thermal resistance in a heat exchanger, considering fouling, is given by:

$$1/U_f = 1/U + R_{f,hot} + R_{f,cold}$$

Where:
- U_f is the overall heat transfer coefficient with fouling,
- U is the overall heat transfer coefficient without fouling,
- $R_{f,hot}$ and $R_{f,cold}$ are fouling resistances on the hot and cold fluid sides, respectively.

Fouling leads to increased energy consumption and maintenance frequency. Therefore, fouling factors are incorporated into design calculations to ensure reliable operation over time.

2. Effectiveness of Heat Exchanger

The effectiveness (ε) of a heat exchanger is a dimensionless parameter that represents the ratio of the actual heat transfer to the maximum possible heat transfer under given conditions. It provides a measure of how efficiently the heat exchanger performs.

$$\varepsilon = q_{actual}/q_{max}$$

Where:
- q_{actual} is the actual rate of heat transfer,
- $q_{max} = C_{min}(T_{h,in} - T_{c,in})$ is the maximum possible heat transfer,
- C_{min} is the minimum heat capacity rate between the hot and cold fluids.

Effectiveness depends on the type of heat exchanger (parallel flow, counterflow, crossflow), the number of passes, and the flow arrangement. It is particularly useful in the effectiveness-NTU method for sizing or performance analysis when outlet temperatures are not known.

3. Correction Factor for Multipass Arrangement

In practical applications, many heat exchangers do not operate in a true counterflow or parallel flow mode but instead have complex configurations like multipass shell-and-tube arrangements. To analyse such systems, a correction factor (F) is introduced in the logarithmic mean temperature difference (LMTD) method.

The corrected LMTD is given by:

$$\Delta T_{corrected} = F \cdot \Delta T_{LMTD}$$

Where: ΔT_{LMTD} is the logarithmic mean temperature difference for ideal counterflow or parallel flow,
- F is the correction factor, typically less than 1.

Q.2   **What do you mean by radiation shield? Give two examples of use of radiation**
A   **shield.**

A radiation shield is a barrier or layer of material designed to reduce or prevent the transfer of thermal radiation from one surface to another. It works by reflecting, absorbing, or scattering the radiative heat energy, thereby minimizing the net heat transfer through radiation. Radiation shields are especially effective in high-temperature environments or vacuum conditions where conduction and convection are negligible.

Examples of Use of Radiation Shields:
1. Cryogenic Storage Systems: In liquid nitrogen or liquid helium storage tanks, radiation shields are used between the inner and outer walls to reduce heat transfer and minimize boil-off of the cryogenic liquid.
2. **Spacecraft Thermal Protection:** Satellites and space vehicles use multi-layer radiation shields to protect sensitive equipment from intense solar radiation and extreme temperatures in space.

B   **With suitable example, explain in brief about black body, white body, opaque body and transparent body.**

Black Body
A black body is an idealized physical object that absorbs all incident electromagnetic radiation, regardless of wavelength or angle of incidence. It neither reflects nor transmits any radiation. It is also a perfect emitter of radiation when heated and radiates energy at the maximum possible rate for a given temperature, as described by Planck's law.
- Example: A cavity with a small hole (black body cavity) is often used in laboratories to simulate black body behavior. The Sun also closely approximates a black body.

White Body
A white body is a theoretical object that reflects all incident radiation and absorbs none. It also does not emit radiation on its own. This concept is used as an ideal opposite to a black body.
- Example: Fresh snow or a highly reflective white painted surface approximates a white body in real-world conditions, though no perfect white body exists in nature.

Opaque Body
An opaque body is one that does not allow radiation to pass through it. Radiation incident on an opaque body is either absorbed or reflected. The transmittance of such a body is zero.
- Example: Metals such as iron or aluminium are opaque bodies as they do not transmit light.

C   **An aluminium fin (k = 200W/mK, 2.5cm long,1m width, and 3.5mm thick) protrudes from a wall. The base is at 420^0C and surrounding air temperature is 30^0C.**
Determine the heat dissipated from the fin and fin efficiency for the fin is of finite length and heat loss from fin tip is negligible.
Take h = 11W/m^{2}K.

- Thermal conductivity, $k = 200\,\mathrm{W/m \cdot K}$

- Fin length, $L = 2.5\,\mathrm{cm} = 0.025\,\mathrm{m}$

- Fin width, $w = 1\,\mathrm{m}$

- Fin thickness, $t = 3.5\,\mathrm{mm} = 0.0035\,\mathrm{m}$

- Base temperature, $T_b = 420^{\circ}C$

- Surrounding air temperature, $T_\infty = 30^{\circ}C$

- Heat transfer coefficient, $h = 11\,\mathrm{W/m^2 \cdot K}$

- Heat loss from fin tip is negligible

Step 1: Calculate the cross-sectional area (A_c) and perimeter (P) of the fin

$$A_c = w \times t = 1 \times 0.0035 = 0.0035\,\mathrm{m^2}$$

$$P = 2 \times (w + t) = 2 \times (1 + 0.0035) = 2.007\,\mathrm{m}$$

Step 2: Calculate the fin parameter m

$$m = \sqrt{\frac{hP}{kA_c}} = \sqrt{\frac{11 \times 2.007}{200 \times 0.0035}}$$

Calculate numerator and denominator:

$$hP = 11 \times 2.007 = 22.077\,\mathrm{W/m^2 \cdot K}$$

$$kA_c = 200 \times 0.0035 = 0.7\,\mathrm{W/K}$$

Now,

$$m = \sqrt{\frac{22.077}{0.7}} = \sqrt{31.53} = 5.615\,\mathrm{m^{-1}}$$

Step 3: Calculate the fin efficiency η_f

For a fin with insulated tip (heat loss from fin tip is negligible), fin efficiency is:

$$\eta_f = \frac{\tanh(mL)}{mL}$$

Calculate mL:

$$mL = 5.615 \times 0.025 = 0.1404$$
$$\tanh(0.1404) \approx 0.1395$$

Therefore,

$$\eta_f = \frac{0.1395}{0.1404} = 0.9936$$

Step 4: Calculate heat dissipated from the fin (Q_f)

Heat dissipation from the fin is given by:

$$Q_f = \sqrt{hPkA_c}(T_b - T_\infty)\tanh(mL)$$

Calculate the term $\sqrt{hPkA_c}$:

$$hP = 22.077, \quad kA_c = 0.7$$

$$hPkA_c = 22.077 \times 0.7 = 15.454$$

$$\sqrt{15.454} = 3.931\ \text{W/K}$$

Calculate temperature difference:

$$\Delta T = T_b - T_\infty = 420 - 30 = 390°C$$

Finally,

$$Q_f = 3.931 \times 390 \times 0.1395 = 213.5\ \text{W}$$

OR

C   **A furnace wall, 32 cm thick, is made up of an inner layer of brick (k=0.84W/mK) covered with a layer of insulation (k=0.16W/mK).**
The furnace operates at a temperature of 1325⁰C and the ambient temperature is 25⁰C.
  i) Determine the thickness of brick and insulation which gives minimum heat loss, Calculate the heat loss presuming that the insulating material has a maximum temperature of 1200⁰C.
If the calculated heat loss is not accepted than state whether addition of another layer of insulation would provide a satisfactory solution.

    Given data : $t_1 = 1325°C, t_3 = 25°C, t_2 = 1200°C, k_B = 0.16W/mK,$

$k_A = 0.84W/mK, \quad q = ?$

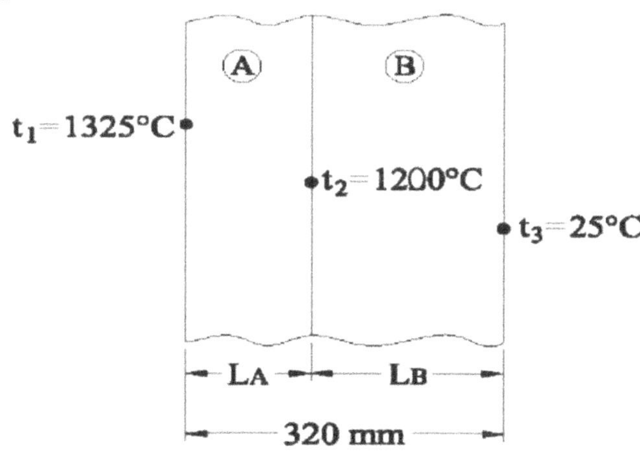

Figure

$$q = \frac{t_1 - t_3}{\dfrac{L_A}{K_A} + \dfrac{L_B}{K_B}} = \frac{t_1 - t_2}{\dfrac{L_A}{K_A}} = \frac{t_2 - t_3}{\dfrac{L_B}{K_B}}$$

considering first two parameters,

$$\frac{(1325 - 25)}{\dfrac{L_A}{0.84} + \dfrac{L_B}{0.16}} = \frac{(1325 - 1200)}{\dfrac{L_A}{0.84}}$$

also, $L_A + L_B = 0.32$

$$\therefore L_A = \frac{210}{(1300 + 531.5)} = 0.1146\,m = 114.6\,mm$$

$\therefore L_B = $ thickness of insulation $= L_B = 320 - 114.6 = 205.4$ mm

$\Rightarrow$ heat loss per unit area,

$$q = \frac{t_1 - t_2}{\dfrac{L_A}{K_A}} = 916.23\,W/m^2$$

If another layer of insulating material is added, the heat loss from the wall will reduce;

consequently the temperature drop across the fire brick lining will drop and the interface temperature will rise. As the interface temperature is already fixed, therefore, satisfactory solution will not be available by adding another layer of insulation.

Q.3 **A) Explain mean film temperature and bulk mean temperature.**
The mean film temperature is the average temperature between the surface and the surrounding fluid. Used to evaluate fluid properties (like viscosity, thermal conductivity, etc.) when calculating heat transfer coefficients in convection.
The bulk mean temperature is the average temperature of the fluid flowing through a pipe or duct, weighted by mass flow rate or energy flow. Used in calculating heat transfer between a flowing fluid and a surface, especially in forced convection.

Key Differences:

Aspect	Mean Film Temperature (Tf)	Bulk Mean Temperature (Tm)
Used For	Evaluating fluid properties for calculations	Energy balance in flowing fluids
Based On	Surface and ambient temperatures	Cross-sectional average temperature of flowing fluid
Typical Application	Free and forced convection	Internal flows (pipes, ducts, channels)

B **Differentiate between boiling and condensation.**

Aspect	Boiling	Condensation
Definition	Boiling is the process where a liquid change to vapor when it reaches its boiling point.	Condensation is the process where vapor changes into a liquid when cooled below its saturation temperature.
Phase Change	Liquid → Vapor	Vapor → Liquid
Heat Involvement	Heat is absorbed by the liquid to cause vaporization.	Heat is released as the vapor condenses to liquid.
Occurs When	The liquid temperature reaches its boiling point.	The vapor temperature drops below the dew point or saturation temperature.
Direction of Heat Flow	Into the substance (heating)	Out of the substance (cooling)
Examples	Boiling water on a stove.	Water droplets forming on a cold glass surface.

C **Discuss the electrical analogy for radiant heat transfer.**

An electrical network analogy is an alternative approach for analysing radiation heat exchange between any surfaces (black or non-black).

From equation (33), $\dfrac{1-\varepsilon}{A\varepsilon}$ is known as surface resistance and it is related to surface properties of radiating body.

From equation (34a), $\dfrac{1}{A_1 \cdot F_{1-2}}$ is known as space resistance which is related to distance and geometry of radiating bodies.

Refer figure no. 12. The electrical circuit for that system is shown in figure no. 13.

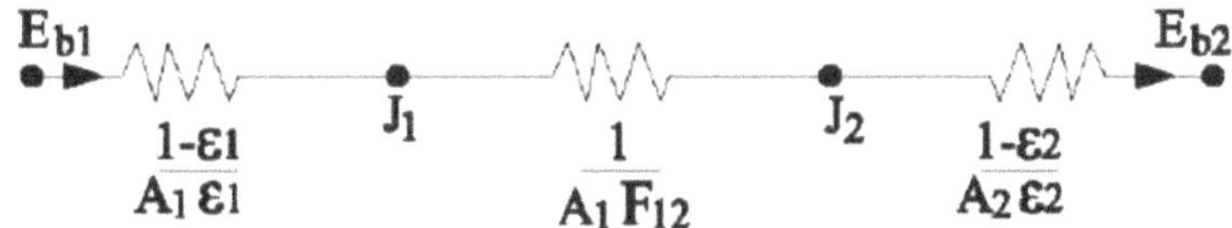

Figure 13 : Electrical network for two parallel plane

So, the net heat exchange between two non-black bodies is given by

$$\left(Q_{1-2}\right)_{Net} = \frac{E_{b1}-E_{b2}}{\dfrac{1-\varepsilon_1}{A_1\varepsilon_1}+\dfrac{1}{A_1 F_{12}}+\dfrac{1-\varepsilon_2}{A_2\varepsilon_2}}$$

$$= \frac{\sigma \cdot A_1 \cdot \left(T_1^4 - T_2^4\right)}{\dfrac{1-\varepsilon_1}{\varepsilon_1}+\dfrac{1}{F_{12}}+\dfrac{1-\varepsilon_2}{\varepsilon_2}\cdot\dfrac{A_1}{A_2}}$$

$$\therefore Q_{12} = \frac{(1)}{\frac{1-\varepsilon_1}{\varepsilon_1} + \frac{1}{F_{12}} + \frac{1-\varepsilon_2}{\varepsilon_2}\frac{A_1}{A_2}} \left[\sigma A_1 \left(T_1^4 - T_2^4\right)\right]$$

$$Q_{12} = \left(f_g\right)_{1-2} \sigma \cdot A_1 \cdot \left(T_1^4 - T_2^4\right) \qquad \qquad ...(40)$$

$\left(f_g\right)_{1-2}$ is known as gray body factor.

Equation (40) is the most general equation for the two non-black bodies which are exchanging the heat.

OR

Q.3 **Justify that a good absorber is also a good emitter for radiation heat transfer.**

The principle that a good absorber is also a good emitter of radiation in heat transfer is justified by Kirchhoff's Law of Thermal Radiation, which states:

At thermal equilibrium, the emissivity of a material (its effectiveness in emitting energy as radiation) is equal to its absorptivity (its effectiveness in absorbing radiation) for a given wavelength and temperature.

According to Kirchhoff's Law, at thermal equilibrium, the emissivity (ε) of a surface is equal to its absorptivity (α) for a given wavelength and temperature:

$\varepsilon = \alpha$

This means that a material that absorbs radiation well at a particular wavelength and temperature will also emit radiation efficiently under the same conditions.

B **Explain in detail about cross flow heat exchanger with its advantages. Give suitable examples.**

A cross-flow heat exchanger is a type of heat exchanger where two fluids flow perpendicular to each other—one flows through a set of tubes or fins, and the other flows across those tubes/fins.

This setup allows heat to be transferred between fluids without them mixing, making it highly effective in applications where fluids must remain separate.

advantages of cross flow heat exchangers:

- Compact and space-saving design
- Effective for air-liquid heat exchange
- Customizable for single or multi-pass flow
- Cost-effective and easy to manufacture
- Simple to maintain and clean
- Suitable for a wide range of industrial and automotive applications

Examples;

1. Automobile Radiators:
   - Coolant (liquid) flows inside tubes, air flows across the tubes.
   - Heat is removed from the engine coolant by the ambient air.
2. Air Conditioning Systems (HVAC):
   - Refrigerant or chilled water flows inside coils.
   - Air is forced over the coils by a fan, allowing cooling of the air.
3. Industrial Cooling Towers:
   - Water flows through tubes or plates.
   - Air flows perpendicularly to cool the water.

4. Waste Heat Recovery Units:
   o Exhaust gases transfer heat to incoming air streams in industrial furnaces.

C **Define condensation process. Also explain film condensation and drop- wise condensation.**

Condensation is the process of a vapor changing into a liquid when it comes into contact with a surface or a region at a lower temperature than the vapor's saturation temperature. This occurs when the vapor loses enough thermal energy (heat) to undergo a phase change.

Condensation is an important mechanism in heat transfer, especially in systems like steam turbines, condensers, refrigeration systems, and heat exchangers.

Types of Condensation

There are two primary types of condensation on surfaces:

1. Film Condensation: Film condensation occurs when the condensed liquid forms a continuous film over the surface.

Characteristics:
- The liquid film covers the surface completely.
- This film acts as a resistance to heat transfer because it adds a thermal layer.
- Common in clean and smooth surfaces.

Heat Transfer: Lower compared to drop-wise condensation due to the thermal resistance of the liquid film.

Example: Condensation on the surface of a cold-water pipe in a humid environment.

2. Drop-wise Condensation: Drop-wise condensation occurs when vapor condenses into individual droplets that do not merge into a film.

Characteristics:
- Droplets form and fall off, exposing the surface repeatedly to fresh vapor.
- Occurs on hydrophobic or specially coated surfaces.
- The bare metal surface remains exposed more frequently.

Heat Transfer: Significantly higher heat transfer coefficient than film condensation (up to 5–10 times more efficient).

Example: Condensation on a freshly waxed or coated glass surface.

Q.4 **'It is desirable to use two thin fins instead of one thick fin for engine cooling'.**
A   **Give reason.**

It is desirable to use two thin fins instead of one thick fin for engine cooling because two thin fins provide a greater surface area for heat transfer, which enhances the rate of convective cooling. Thin fins also have a shorter conduction path, allowing heat to transfer more efficiently from the base to the tip. Additionally, thin fins maintain a higher temperature gradient, resulting in better fin efficiency compared to a thick fin, which may lose effectiveness toward its tip due to a reduced temperature difference. Using multiple thin fins also improves airflow between the fins, aiding in better heat dissipation, whereas a thick fin can obstruct airflow. Therefore, two thin fins offer more effective and efficient engine cooling than a single thick fin.

B **What is insulation? State its four applications in engineering field.**

Insulation refers to a material or method used to reduce the transfer of heat, sound, or electricity between objects or environments. In thermal applications, insulation is primarily used to minimize heat loss or gain, helping maintain desired temperatures and improve energy efficiency.

Insulating materials typically have low thermal conductivity, meaning they resist the flow of heat.

Four Applications of Insulation in Engineering:

1. Thermal Insulation in Buildings
    - Used in walls, roofs, and floors to prevent heat loss in winter and heat gain in summer.
    - Improves energy efficiency and reduces heating/cooling costs.
2. Pipe and Duct Insulation
    - Applied to steam, hot water, and chilled water pipes in power plants, HVAC systems, and industries.
    - Minimizes heat loss/gain, prevents condensation, and improves system performance.
3. Electrical Insulation
    - Used in wires, cables, transformers, and motors to prevent electrical leakage and ensure safety.
    - Common materials: rubber, plastic, mica, or ceramic.
4. Insulation in Refrigeration and Cryogenics
    - Used in refrigerators, freezers, and cryogenic tanks to reduce heat influx, maintaining low internal temperatures.
    - Essential for storing liquefied gases like liquid nitrogen or oxygen.

C **Write the most general equation in Cartesian co-ordinates for heat transfer by conduction. Deduce above equation for the following cases with suitable assumptions; (i) Laplace equation, (ii) Poisson equation, and (iii) Fourier equation.**

$$\frac{\partial^2 t}{\partial x^2} + \frac{\partial^2 t}{\partial y^2} + \frac{\partial^2 t}{\partial z^2} + \frac{\dot{q}_g}{k} = \frac{\rho.c}{k} \cdot \frac{\partial t}{\partial \tau} = \frac{1}{\alpha} \cdot \frac{\partial t}{\partial \tau} \qquad \text{...(15-a)}$$

Equation (15-a) by using Laplacian ∇^2, may be written as :

$$\nabla^2 t + \frac{\dot{q}_g}{k} = \frac{1}{\alpha} \cdot \frac{\partial t}{\partial \tau} \qquad \text{...(16)}$$

Equations (15-a) and (16) are known as equations for heat conduction with internal heat generation for three dimensional system under unsteady state, applicable to all the isotropic/ homogneous material in Cartesian coordinate system.

1.4.2 Other simplified forms of heat conduction equations :

Case (i) When no internal source of heat generation is present, Eqn. (15-a) reduces to

$$\frac{\partial^2 t}{\partial x^2} + \frac{\partial^2 t}{\partial y^2} + \frac{\partial^2 t}{\partial z^2} = \frac{1}{\alpha} \cdot \frac{\partial t}{\partial \tau} \qquad \text{...(17)}$$

or, using Laplacian ∇^2,

$$\nabla^2 t = \frac{1}{\alpha} \cdot \frac{\partial t}{\partial \tau} \quad \text{(Fourier's equation)} \qquad \text{...(18)}$$

Case (ii) When the conduction then takes place in the steady state $\left(i.e. \frac{\partial t}{\partial \tau} = 0 \right)$, the equation (15-a) reduces to,

$$\frac{\partial^2 t}{\partial x^2} + \frac{\partial^2 t}{\partial y^2} + \frac{\partial^2 t}{\partial z^2} + \frac{\dot{q}_g}{k} = 0 \qquad \text{...(19)}$$

$$\nabla^2 t + \frac{\dot{q_g}}{k} = 0 \ \text{(Poisson's equation)} \qquad \text{...(20)}$$

In the absence of internal heat generation, Eqn. (20) reduces to

$$\frac{\partial^2 t}{\partial x^2} + \frac{\partial^2 t}{\partial y^2} + \frac{\partial^2 t}{\partial z^2} = 0 \qquad \text{...(21)}$$

or, $\nabla^2 t = 0$ (Laplace equation) $\qquad \text{...(22)}$

OR

Q.4 **A) Use of aluminum material as a cooking utensil are not desirable. Evaluate.**

Aluminium is widely used in cookware due to its excellent thermal conductivity, light weight, and low cost. However, there are several concerns that make its use in cooking utensils less desirable in certain situations:

1. Reactivity with Food: Aluminium is a highly reactive metal. It can react with acidic or salty foods, such as tomatoes or vinegar-based dishes, leading to a metallic taste and potential leaching of aluminium into the food. This may raise health concerns over long-term exposure.

2. Health Concerns: Although scientific studies have not conclusively proven that aluminium causes health issues like Alzheimer's disease, the possibility of aluminium accumulation in the body has raised public concern. This has led many to avoid uncoated aluminium cookware.

3. Durability: Aluminium is a soft metal and can easily warp or scratch. When scratched, more aluminium is exposed to food, increasing the chances of chemical interaction.

4. Staining and Discoloration: Aluminium cookware often stains and discolors with time, especially when used with certain ingredients or under high heat, affecting its appearance and sometimes its functionality.

While aluminum has advantages in terms of heat transfer and cost, its direct use in cooking utensils can be undesirable due to chemical reactivity and health concerns.

B **Write the general differential equation in Cartesian co-ordinates for 3-D unsteady heat conduction by considering an infinitesimal volume element. Deduce there from the conduction equations for the following cases;**
   (i) **Steady state 1-D flow with heat generation at uniform rate within material,**
   (ii) **Steady 2-D flow without heat generation.**

$$\frac{\partial^2 t}{\partial x^2} + \frac{\partial^2 t}{\partial y^2} + \frac{\partial^2 t}{\partial z^2} + \frac{\dot{q_g}}{k} = \frac{\rho . c}{k} \cdot \frac{\partial t}{\partial \tau} = \frac{1}{\alpha} \cdot \frac{\partial t}{\partial \tau} \qquad \text{...(15-a)}$$

Equation (15-a) by using Laplacian ∇^2, may be written as :

$$\nabla^2 t + \frac{q_g}{k} = \frac{1}{\alpha} \cdot \frac{\partial t}{\partial \tau} \qquad \qquad ...(16)$$

Equations (15-a) and (16) are known as equations for heat conduction with internal heat generation for three dimensional system under unsteady state, applicable to all the isotropic/ homogneous material in Cartesian coordinate system.

i)Steady state 1-D flow with heat generation at uniform rate within material,

$$\frac{\partial^2 t}{\partial x^2} + \frac{\dot{q}_g}{k} = 0$$

(ii) Steady 2-D flow without heat generation.

$$\frac{\partial^2 t}{\partial x^2} + \frac{\partial^2 t}{\partial y^2} = 0$$

C **Explain physical significance of critical radius of insulation and derive an expression for the same critical radius in case of cylinder.**

The critical radius of insulation refers to a unique concept in heat transfer, particularly in cylindrical or spherical systems such as pipes and wires. This occurs due to the combined effects of conduction through the insulation material and convection from the outer surface to the surrounding environment. Adding insulation increases resistance to conduction, which is desirable, but it also increases the surface area exposed to convection, which can increase heat loss.

Consider a layer of insulation of thermal conductivity k, applied on a solid circular cylinder of radius r_1 (figure no. 16)

For the solid cylinder

Let, L = Length of the cylinder : m

$\qquad t_1$ = surface temperature of solid cylinder : $^{\circ}C$

$\qquad t_{air}$ = air temperature, $^{\circ}C$

$\qquad h_{air}$ = convective heat transfer coefficient for air: W/m^2K

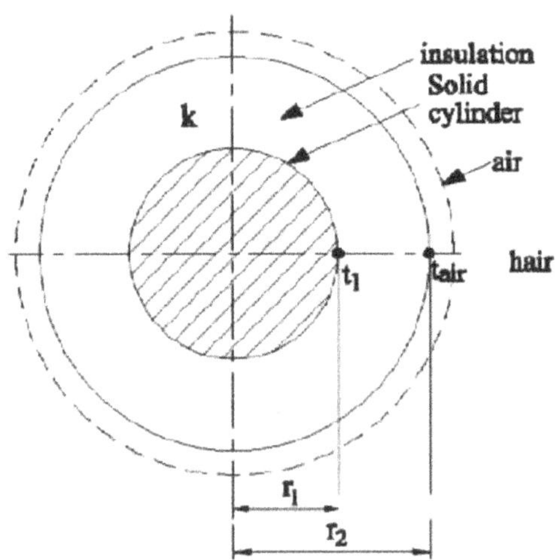

Figure 16 : Critical thickness of insulation for solid cylinder

k = thermal conductivity of insulating material: $W/m\text{-}k$. The rate of heat transfer from solid cylinder to surrounding is given by.

$$Q = \frac{\left(t_1 - t_{air}\right)}{\dfrac{1}{2\pi k \cdot L}\ln\dfrac{r_2}{r_1} + \dfrac{1}{2\pi r_2 L \cdot h_{air}}} \qquad \text{...(31)}$$

from equation (31), $\dfrac{1}{2\pi r_2 L \cdot h_{air}}$ = convection resistance which decreases due to increase in outer radius.

$$\frac{1}{2\pi k \cdot L}\ln\frac{r_2}{r_1} + \frac{1}{2\pi r_2 L \cdot h_{air}} = \text{total thermal resistance} \qquad \text{...(32)}$$

The heat transfer from the solid cylinder (Q) is maximum when the total resistance offered to the heat flow is minimum (i.e. denominator). So differentiate the denominator with respect to r_2 (outer radius) and equate it with zero.

i.e. $\dfrac{d}{dr_2} = \left[\dfrac{1}{2\pi kL}\ln\dfrac{r_2}{r_1} + \dfrac{1}{2\pi r_2 L \cdot h_{air}}\right] = 0$

$$(\because r_2 \text{ being the only variable}).$$

$$\therefore \frac{1}{k}\cdot\frac{1}{r_2} + \frac{1}{h_{air}}\left(-\frac{1}{r_2^2}\right) = 0$$

$$\frac{1}{k}\cdot\frac{1}{r_2} = \frac{1}{r_2^2}\cdot\frac{1}{h_{air}}$$

$$\therefore h_{air}\cdot r_2 = k$$

$$\therefore r_2 = r_c = \frac{k}{h_{air}} \qquad \text{...(33)}$$

Equation (33) represent the radius upto which heat transfer is maximum (i.e. resistance offered to the heat transfer is minimum). So when radius for the cylinder has value less than or equals to the critical radius $\left(r_c\right)$, heat transfer rate tends to increase or become maximum. If radius of insulation over the cylinder is more than r_c (critical radius) then the heat transfer start to decrease.

Equation (33) represents the condition for minimum resistance and maximum heat flow rate.

Q.5   A) Differentiate natural and forced convection.

Natural Convection	Forced Convection
Heat transfers due to natural fluid motion caused by buoyancy forces from density differences.	Heat transfers due to fluid motion induced by external means like fans or pumps.
Temperature-induced density variations causing natural circulation.	External devices create fluid flow.

Generally slower and less controlled.	Typically, faster and controllable.
Warm air rising near a heater.	Air forced over a hot surface by a fan.
Usually, lower compared to forced convection.	Usually, higher due to increased fluid velocity.

B   **State the similarities and difference between:**
     1) **Nusselt number and Biot number,**
     2) **Grashoff Number and Reynold number.**

1) Nusselt Number vs. Biot Number

Aspect	Nusselt Number (Nu)	Biot Number (Bi)
Definition	Ratio of convective to conductive heat transfer across a fluid layer	Ratio of internal conduction resistance to external convection resistance
Medium	Involves properties of the fluid	Involves both solid and fluid properties
Purpose	Used in analyzing convection heat transfer in fluids	Used to determine if a solid body can be modeled with lumped system analysis
Indicates	Efficiency of convection at a surface	Relative importance of conduction within solid vs. convection outside
Similarity	Both involve convection heat transfer coefficient (h) and characteristic length	

2) Grashoff Number vs. Reynolds Number

Aspect	Grashoff Number (Gr)	Reynolds Number (Re)
Definition	Ratio of buoyancy to viscous forces in natural convection	Ratio of inertial to viscous forces in forced convection
Flow Type	Governs natural convection	Governs forced convection
Driving Force	Temperature-induced buoyancy	External forces or fluid motion
Purpose	Predicts transition from laminar to turbulent flow in natural convection	Same for forced convection
Similarity	Both are used to characterize fluid flow regimes and influence heat transfer behavior	

C   **What is the limitation of Rayleigh's method of dimensional analysis? Which method is preferred in such case and how repeating variables are selected?**

Rayleigh's method is a basic dimensional analysis technique that expresses a physical quantity as a function of other variables using dimensional homogeneity. It works well when the number of variables involved is small (typically 3–4), but it has a key limitation:

Rayleigh's method becomes inadequate when many variables (5 or more) are involved, especially when:

- The relationship among variables is complex or nonlinear
- Multiple dimensionless groups (π terms) need to be formed
- It's difficult to determine how many independent dimensionless parameters exist.

In such cases, it's not systematic enough and lacks a general procedure for solving problems with multiple variables.

When Rayleigh's method is insufficient, the Buckingham π-theorem is preferred. It provides a systematic approach to dimensional analysis and can handle multiple variables and dimensions efficiently.

To form dimensionless π terms using Buckingham's method, you must select a set of repeating variables. These are used to construct the π terms and should follow certain rules:

☐ Number of repeating variables = Number of fundamental dimensions involved (e.g., M, L, T $\rightarrow$ usually 3 repeating variables),

☐ Include variables that cover all fundamental dimensions, So that all dimensional units are represented.

☐ Avoid using the dependent variable as a repeating variable

☐ Prefer variables with simple physical meaning, like:
- Geometric quantities (length, diameter)
- Flow properties (velocity, density, viscosity)

☐ Do not pick two variables of the same dimension (e.g., don't choose both velocity and acceleration)

OR

Q.5 A) Define: Nusselt number, Grashoff Number and Reynold number.

The Nusselt number is the ratio of convective to conductive heat transfer across a fluid boundary layer. It indicates the enhancement of heat transfer through a fluid layer due to convection compared to pure conduction.

The Grashoff number is the ratio of buoyancy to viscous forces in a fluid, governing natural convection flow. It predicts the onset of natural convection due to temperature differences in the fluid.

The Reynolds number is the ratio of inertial forces to viscous forces in fluid flow. It determines whether the flow is laminar or turbulent.

B State the governing law for convection heat transfer. Explain in brief about convection heat transfer coefficient.

The governing law for convection heat transfer is Newton's Law of Cooling, which states that the rate of heat transfer between a solid surface and a fluid is proportional to the surface area and the temperature difference between the surface and the fluid. Mathematically, it is expressed as:

$$Q = h \cdot A \cdot (T_s - T_\infty)$$

where:
- Q = heat transfer rate (W)
- h = convection heat transfer coefficient (W/m²·K)
- A = surface area (m²)
- T_s = surface temperature (°C or K)
- T_∞ = fluid temperature far from the surface (°C or K)

Convection Heat Transfer Coefficient (h);

The convection heat transfer coefficient, h, quantifies the heat transfer between a surface and a moving fluid per unit area and per unit temperature difference. It depends on several factors such as:
- Fluid properties (thermal conductivity, viscosity, density, specific heat)
- Flow characteristics (velocity, turbulence, laminar or turbulent flow)
- Nature of convection (natural or forced convection)
- Surface geometry and orientation

A higher h value indicates more efficient heat transfer. Typical values of h range from about 5–25 W/m²·K for natural convection in air to several thousand for forced convection in liquids.

C **Using Buckingham–π theorem show that, $Nu = f\ (Re,\ Pr)$ for forced convection.**

Here the different methods of solving the above example is shown :

Using M-L-T-θ system, the dimensions of various quanties can be obtained as under :

(If we want to use M-L-T-θ-H system here we need to consider one more quantity temperature difference Δt and then solve further. This difficulty will not arise in case of free convection because there Δt itself is given as quantity, refer next example)*

Quantity	Symbol	Dimension
Heat Transfer co-efficient	h	$MT^{-3}\theta^{-1}$
Fluid Density	ρ	ML^{-3}
Length	l	L
Fluid Velocity	V	LT^{-1}
Fluid Viscosity	μ	$ML^{-1}T^{-1}$
Specific heat	C_p	$L^2T^{-2}\theta^{-1}$
Thermal conductivity	k	$MLT^{-3}\theta^{-1}$

→ Buckingham's π-theorem :

Total no. of quantities, $n = 7$ and Total no. of fundamental quantities, $m = 4$

∴ No. of π-constants $= n - m = 7 - 4 = 3$.

For obtaining π-groups, we would select length l (geometric), velocity V (flow characteristic), density ρ (fluid property) and thermal conductivity k (thermal property) as repeating variables.

π_1 - **terms** : $\pi_1 = l^{a_1}\ V^{b_1}\ \rho^{c_1}\ k^{d_1}\ h$

$$M^o L^o T^o \theta^o = [L]^{a_1} \left[LT^{-1}\right]^{b_1} \left[ML^{-3}\right]^{c_1} \left[MLT^{-3}\theta^{-1}\right]^{d_1} \left[MT^{-3}\theta^{-1}\right]$$

Equating exponents of $M.L.T.\theta$ we get

For M : $\quad 0 \quad = c_1 + d_1 + 1$

$\quad$ L : $\quad 0 \quad = a_1 + b_1 - 3c_1 + d_1$

$\quad$ T : $\quad 0 \quad = -b_1 - 3\,d_1 - 3$

$\quad$ θ : $\quad 0 \quad = -d_1 - 1$

Equating above equations we get

$a_1 = 1,\ b_1 = 0,\ c_1 = 0,\ d_1 = -1$

Thus, $\qquad \pi_1 = l^1 V^0 \rho^0 k^{-1} h = \dfrac{hl}{k}$

π_2 -**term** : $\pi_2 = l^{a_2} V^{b_2} \rho^{c_2} k^{d_2} \mu$

Putting dimensions,

$$M^o L^o T^o \theta^o = [L]^{a_2} \left[LT^{-1}\right]^{b_2} \left[ML^{-3}\right]^{c_2} \left[MLT^{-3}\theta^{-1}\right]^{d_2} \left[ML^{-1}T^{-1}\right]$$

Equating exponents

For M : $0 \quad = c_2 + d_2 + 1$

L : $0 \quad = a_2 + b_2 - 3c_2 + d_2 - 1$

T : $0 \quad = -b_2 - 3d_2 - 1$

θ : $0 \quad = -d_2$

Equating above equations we get,

$$a_2 = -1, \ b_2 = -1, \ c_2 = -1, \ d_2 = 0$$

Thus, $\pi_2 = l^{-1} V^{-1} \rho^{-1} k^0 \mu = \dfrac{\mu}{\rho V l}$

π_3 -**term** : $\pi_3 = l^{a_3} V^{b_3} \rho^{c_3} k^{d_3} C_p$

$$M^o L^o T^o \theta^o = [L]^{a_3} \left[LT^{-1} \right]^{b_3} \left[ML^{-3} \right]^{c_3} \left[MLT^{-3}\theta^{-1} \right]^{d_3} \left[L^2 T^{-2}\theta^{-1} \right]$$

Equating exponents :

For M : $0 \quad = c_3 + d_3$

L : $0 \quad = a_3 + b_3 - 3c_3 + d_3 + 2$

T : $0 \quad = -b_3 - 3d_3 - 2$

θ : $0 \quad = -d_3 - 1$

Equating above equations we get,

$$a_3 = 1, \ b_3 = 1, \ c_3 = 1, \ d_3 = -1$$

Thus, $\pi_3 = l^1 v^1 \rho^1 k^{-1} C_p = \dfrac{\rho v l}{k} \times C_p$

Now, this not popular dimensionless group. (or Prandtl No.)

Equating the dimensions of $\rho v l$ we get

$$\left[ML^{-3} \right]\left[LT^{-1} \right][L] = ML^{-1}T^{-1}$$

which is the dimension of viscosity μ, so we can use μ in place of $\rho v l$.

$$\therefore \pi_3 = \dfrac{\mu C_p}{k} \quad \text{(or Prandtl No.)}$$

Now considering $\phi(\pi_1, \pi_2, \pi_3) = 0$ or $\phi\left(\dfrac{hl}{k} \cdot \dfrac{\mu}{\rho v l} \cdot \dfrac{\mu C_p}{k} \right) = 0$

or $\dfrac{hl}{k} = \phi\left(\dfrac{\mu}{\rho v l} \cdot \dfrac{\mu C_p}{k} \right)$

or $\dfrac{hl}{k} = \phi\left(\dfrac{\rho v l}{\mu} \cdot \dfrac{\mu C_p}{k} \right)$

or $Nu = \phi(Re, Pr)$

PAPER 4_ 3151909: HEAT TRANSFER

WINTER 2022 EXAM   DATE: 06/01/2023

Q.1 **Define the conduction, convection and radiation modes of heat transfer with suitable**
A   **example.**
1. Conduction: Conduction is the transfer of heat through a solid material from one molecule to another without any movement of the material as a whole. It occurs due to the vibration and interaction of particles in a solid.
Example: When a metal rod is heated at one end, the heat travels through the rod to the other end. If you touch the other end after a while, it becomes hot due to conduction.
2. Convection: Convection is the transfer of heat by the movement of a fluid (liquid or gas). It occurs when the warmer part of the fluid rises and the cooler part sinks, setting up a circulation pattern.
Example: water in a pot: the water at the bottom gets heated, becomes less dense, rises, and cooler water descends to take its place, creating a convection current.
3. Radiation: Radiation is the transfer of heat in the form of electromagnetic waves (usually infrared), without needing any medium. It can occur even in a vacuum.
Example: The Sun heating the Earth: Heat travels through the vacuum of space via radiation.

B   **Describe the thermal conductivity and explain its significance in heat Transfer.**
Thermal conductivity (k) is a material property that measures a material's ability to conduct heat. It quantifies how efficiently heat is transferred through a material due to a temperature gradient.
Physical Meaning:
- A high thermal conductivity means heat flows easily through the material (e.g., metals like copper or aluminium).
- A low thermal conductivity means the material resists heat flow (e.g., insulators like wood, rubber, or fiberglass).

Significance in Heat Transfer:
1. Material Selection:
   - In cooking utensils, materials with high thermal conductivity (like aluminium or copper) are used for faster heat transfer.
   - In building insulation, materials with low thermal conductivity (like foam or fiberglass) reduce heat loss or gain.
2. Electronics Cooling:
   - Electronic devices use heat sinks made of high k materials to dissipate heat efficiently and prevent overheating.
3. Thermal Insulation Design:
   - Used in thermal protection systems in spacecraft, refrigerators, or cold storage units to maintain temperature by minimizing heat flow.
4. Engineering Calculations:
   - Accurate knowledge of k is essential for designing heat exchangers, pipes, boilers, etc.

C   **A steel fin (k = 54 W/mK) with a cross section of an equilateral triangle, 5 mm in side and 80 mm long. It is attached to a plane wall maintained at 400°C. The ambient air temperature is 50°C and convective heat transfer coefficient at surface is 90 W/m²K.**

Calculate the heat dissipation rate from the rod. Assume the fin is of infinite long.

- $h = 90\,\mathrm{W/m^2 K}$ = convective heat transfer coefficient
- P = perimeter of the cross-section
- $k = 54\,\mathrm{W/mK}$ = thermal conductivity of steel
- A_c = cross-sectional area
- $T_b = 400^\circ\mathrm{C}$ = base temperature
- $T_\infty = 50^\circ\mathrm{C}$ = ambient temperature

Step 1: Geometry of Equilateral Triangle

Side of triangle = 5 mm = 0.005 m

Perimeter:

$$P = 3 \times \text{side} = 3 \times 0.005 = 0.015\,\mathrm{m}$$

Area:

$$A_c = \frac{\sqrt{3}}{4} \cdot \text{side}^2 = \frac{\sqrt{3}}{4} \cdot (0.005)^2 = 1.0825 \times 10^{-5}\,\mathrm{m^2}$$

Step 2: Substitute in the Formula

$$Q_{\text{fin}} = \sqrt{hPkA_c} \cdot (T_b - T_\infty)$$

Substitute values:

$$Q_{\text{fin}} = \sqrt{90 \cdot 0.015 \cdot 54 \cdot 1.0825 \times 10^{-5}} \cdot (400 - 50)$$

First compute the value inside the square root:

$$= \sqrt{90 \cdot 0.015 \cdot 54 \cdot 1.0825 \times 10^{-5}}$$
$$= \sqrt{0.0007886} \approx 0.02807$$

Now:

$$Q_{\text{fin}} = 0.02807 \cdot 350 = 9.82\,\mathrm{W}$$

Q.2 A) Define fin efficiency and fin effectiveness.

1.Fin Efficiency

Fin efficiency is the ratio of the actual heat transferred by the fin to the heat that would be transferred if the entire fin were at the base (wall) temperature.

☐ Fin efficiency shows how effectively a fin conducts heat relative to an ideal case.

☐ Always less than or equal to 1.

☐ Higher efficiency means the fin material has good thermal conductivity and is not too long (minimizing temperature drop along the fin).

2. Fin Effectiveness

Fin effectiveness is the ratio of the heat transfer with the fin to the heat transfer that would occur without the fin from the same base area.

☐ Tells whether the use of a fin is beneficial.

☐ If $\varepsilon_{\text{fin}} > 1 \rightarrow$ the fin improves heat transfer.

B **Give eight examples related to heat transfer from the routine life.**

1. Cooking on a Stove (Conduction): Heat is transferred from the burner to the metal pan through direct contact, and then from the pan to the food via conduction.
2. Boiling Water (Convection): As water heats up, the hot water rises and cooler water sinks, creating convection currents that distribute heat evenly.
3. Sunlight Warming Your Skin (Radiation): The Sun transfers heat to your body via electromagnetic waves (infrared radiation), even though the vacuum of space.
4. Ironing Clothes (Conduction): The hot soleplate of the iron transfers heat directly to the fabric, smoothing out wrinkles through conduction.
5. Air Conditioner Cooling a Room (Convection): Cool air circulates and removes warm air through forced convection, distributing cooler temperatures evenly in a room.
6. Hot Coffee Cooling Down (Convection + Radiation): Heat is lost to the surrounding air through natural convection and radiates from the surface of the coffee cup.
7. Wearing a Jacket in Winter (Insulation and Reduced Conduction): A jacket traps air (a poor conductor) and reduces heat loss from your body, keeping you warm.
8. Car Engine Cooling System (Conduction + Convection): Heat from the engine block is transferred to the coolant fluid (conduction), which then carries it to the radiator and releases it to the air via convection.

C **Write the most general equation in Cartesian co-ordinates for heat transfer by conduction. Deduce above equation for the following cases with suitable assumptions;**
   (i)   **Laplace equation,**
   (ii)   **Poisson equation, and**
   (iii) **Fourier equation.**

The general equation for heat transfer by conduction in a three-dimensional, isotropic medium with internal heat generation is given by the **heat conduction equation** (also known as the energy equation). In Cartesian coordinates (x, y, z), it is expressed as:

$$\frac{\partial}{\partial x}\left(k\frac{\partial T}{\partial x}\right) + \frac{\partial}{\partial y}\left(k\frac{\partial T}{\partial y}\right) + \frac{\partial}{\partial z}\left(k\frac{\partial T}{\partial z}\right) + \dot{q} = \rho c_p \frac{\partial T}{\partial t}$$

(i) Laplace Equation

Assumptions:

- Steady-state heat conduction $\left(\frac{\partial T}{\partial t} = 0\right)$

- No internal heat generation $(\dot{q} = 0)$

- Constant thermal conductivity k

Equation reduces to:

$$k \left(\frac{\partial^2 T}{\partial x^2} + \frac{\partial^2 T}{\partial y^2} + \frac{\partial^2 T}{\partial z^2} \right) = 0$$

Dividing by k (since $k \neq 0$):

$$\frac{\partial^2 T}{\partial x^2} + \frac{\partial^2 T}{\partial y^2} + \frac{\partial^2 T}{\partial z^2} = 0$$

This is known as the **Laplace Equation**.
(ii) Poisson Equation

Assumptions:

- Steady-state heat conduction $\left(\frac{\partial T}{\partial t} = 0 \right)$

- Internal heat generation exists $(\dot{q} \neq 0)$

- Constant thermal conductivity k

Equation reduces to:

$$k \left(\frac{\partial^2 T}{\partial x^2} + \frac{\partial^2 T}{\partial y^2} + \frac{\partial^2 T}{\partial z^2} \right) + \dot{q} = 0$$

Dividing by k:

$$\frac{\partial^2 T}{\partial x^2} + \frac{\partial^2 T}{\partial y^2} + \frac{\partial^2 T}{\partial z^2} = -\frac{\dot{q}}{k}$$

This is known as the **Poisson Equation**.

(iii) Fourier Equation

Assumptions:

- Transient (unsteady) heat conduction $\left(\frac{\partial T}{\partial t} \neq 0 \right)$

- No internal heat generation $(\dot{q} = 0)$
- Constant thermal conductivity k

Equation becomes:

$$k \left(\frac{\partial^2 T}{\partial x^2} + \frac{\partial^2 T}{\partial y^2} + \frac{\partial^2 T}{\partial z^2} \right) = \rho c_p \frac{\partial T}{\partial t}$$

Dividing by ρc_p:

$$\frac{\partial T}{\partial t} = \alpha \left(\frac{\partial^2 T}{\partial x^2} + \frac{\partial^2 T}{\partial y^2} + \frac{\partial^2 T}{\partial z^2} \right)$$

Where $\alpha = \frac{k}{\rho c_p}$ is the **thermal diffusivity**.

This is known as the **Fourier Equation** or the **heat diffusion equation**.

C   **Derive general heat conduction equation in cylindrical coordinates.**

While dealing with problems of conduction of heat through systems having cylindrical geometries (e.q. wires, rods and pipes) it is convenient to use cylindrical coordinates (r, ϕ, z).

Consider an element volume having the coordinates (r, ϕ, z), for three-dimensional heat conduction analysis, as shown in Figure 06.

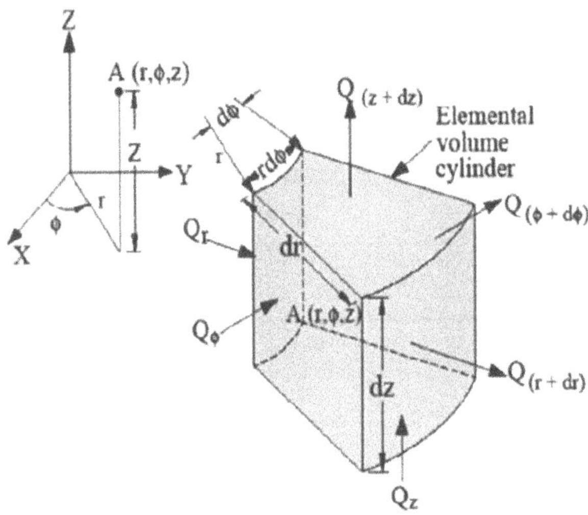

Figure 6 : Elemental volume in Cylindrical coordinates systems

*   Volume of the elemental cylinder $= r . d\phi . dr . dz$
*   For the given cylinder, K = thermal conductivity of the material, c = specific heat,

  ρ = density and $\dot{q}_g$ = heat generation per unit volume per unit time.

A. Net heat accumulated in the cylinder due to conduction of heat.

   – Heat flow in $(x - \phi)$ plane (radial direction) :

Heat influx, $Q'_r = -k\left(rd\phi.dz\right)\dfrac{\partial t}{\partial r}\cdot d\tau$ ..(27)

Heat efflux, $Q'_{(r+dr)} = Q'_r + \dfrac{\partial}{\partial r}\left(Q_r\right)dr$ ..(28)

$\therefore$ Heat accumulation in the cylinder in radial direction,

$$dQ'_r = Q'_r - Q'_{(r+dr)}$$

$$= -\dfrac{\partial}{\partial r}\left(Q'_r\right)dr$$

$$= -\dfrac{\partial}{\partial r}\left[-k\left(rd\phi.dz\right)\dfrac{\partial t}{\partial r}\cdot \partial\tau\right]dr$$

$$= k\left(dr.d\phi.dz\right)\frac{\partial}{\partial r}\left(r\cdot\frac{\partial t}{\partial r}\right)d\tau$$

$$= k\left(dr.d\phi.dz\right)\left(r\frac{\partial^2 t}{\partial r^2}+\frac{\partial t}{\partial r}\right)d\tau$$

$$dQ'_r = k\left(dr.rd\phi.dz\right)\left(\frac{\partial^2 t}{\partial r^2}+\frac{1}{r}\frac{\partial t}{\partial r}\right)d\tau$$

$-$ Heat flow in $(r\text{-}z)$ plane (tangential direction) :

Heat influx, $\quad Q'_\phi = -k\left(dr.dz\right)\dfrac{\partial t}{r.\partial\phi}d\tau$

Heat efflux, $\quad Q'_{(\phi+d\phi)} = Q'_\phi + \dfrac{\partial}{r.\partial\phi}\left(Q'_\phi\right)rd\phi$

Heat accumulated in the element due to heat flow in tangential direction,

$$dQ'_\phi = Q'_\phi - Q'_{(\phi+d\phi)}$$

$$= -\frac{\partial}{r.\partial\phi}\left(Q'_\phi\right)r.d\phi$$

$$= -\frac{\partial}{r.\partial\phi}\left[-k\left(dr.dz\right)\frac{\partial}{r.\partial\phi}\cdot\partial\tau\right]r.d\phi$$

$$= k\left(dr.d\phi.dz\right)\frac{\partial}{\partial\phi}\left(\frac{1}{r}\cdot\frac{\partial t}{\partial\phi}\right)d\tau$$

$$dQ'_\phi = k\left(dr.rd\phi.dz\right)\frac{1}{r^2}\cdot\frac{\partial^2 t}{\partial\phi^2}\cdot d\tau$$

$-$ Heat flow in $(r\text{-}\phi$ plane) (axial direction) :

Heat influx, $\quad Q'_z = -k\left(r.d\phi.dr\right)\dfrac{\partial t}{\partial z}d\tau$

Heat efflux, $\quad Q'_{(z+dz)} = Q'_z + \dfrac{\partial}{\partial z}\left(Q'_z\right)dz$

Heat accumulated due to heat flow in axial direction,

$$dQ'_z = Q'_z - Q'_{(z+dz)}$$

$$= -\frac{\partial}{\partial z}\left[-k\left(r.d\phi.dr\right)\frac{\partial t}{\partial z}\cdot\partial\tau\right]dz$$

$$dQ'_z = k\left(dr.rd\phi.dz\right)\frac{\partial^2 t}{\partial z^2}.d\tau$$

$\therefore$ Heat accumulated in the cylinder,

$$A = k.dr.rd\phi.dz\left[\frac{\partial^2 t}{\partial r^2}+\frac{1}{r}\cdot\frac{\partial t}{\partial r}+\frac{1}{r^2}\cdot\frac{\partial^2 t}{\partial\phi^2}+\frac{\partial^2 t}{\partial z^2}\right]d\tau$$

B. Heat generated within the element $\left(Q'_g\right)$:

The total heat generated

$$B = Q'_g = \dot{q}_g\cdot\left(dr.r.d\phi.dz\right)\cdot d\tau$$

C. Energy stored in the element :

The increase in thermal energy in the element is equal to

$$C = \rho\left(dr.r.d\phi.dz\right).c.\frac{\partial t}{\partial\tau}.d\tau$$

From equation (5), $A + B = C$

$$\therefore k.dr.rd\phi.dz\left[\frac{\partial^2 t}{\partial r^2}+\frac{1}{r}\cdot\frac{\partial t}{\partial r}+\frac{1}{r^2}\cdot\frac{\partial^2 t}{\partial\phi^2}+\frac{\partial^2 t}{\partial z^2}\right]d\tau + \dot{q}_g\left(dr.rd\phi.dz\right).d\tau$$

$$= \rho\left(dr.r.d\phi.dz\right).c.\frac{\partial t}{\partial\tau}.d\tau$$

Dividing both sides by $dr.rd\phi.dz.d\tau$, we have

$$k\left[\frac{\partial^2 t}{\partial r^2}+\frac{1}{r}\cdot\frac{\partial t}{\partial r}+\frac{1}{r^2}\cdot\frac{\partial^2 t}{\partial\phi^2}+\frac{\partial^2 t}{\partial z^2}\right]+\dot{q}_g = \rho.c.\frac{\partial t}{\partial\tau}$$

or
$$\left[\frac{\partial^2 t}{\partial r^2}+\frac{1}{r}\cdot\frac{\partial t}{\partial r}+\frac{1}{r^2}\cdot\frac{\partial^2 t}{\partial\phi^2}+\frac{\partial^2 t}{\partial z^2}\right]+\frac{\dot{q}_g}{k} = \frac{\rho c}{k}\cdot\frac{\partial t}{\partial\tau} = \frac{1}{\alpha}\cdot\frac{\partial t}{\partial\tau}$$

Above equation is the most general equation in the cylindrical co-ordinate system.

Q.3 **A) Define Grashoff number. Explain its significance in natural convection heat transfer.**

The Grashoff number is a dimensionless number used in fluid dynamics and heat transfer to quantify the ratio of buoyancy forces to viscous forces in a fluid. It plays a role in determining the nature and intensity of natural (free) convection.

Physical Significance:
- Buoyancy force arises when a fluid is heated and becomes less dense, causing it to rise and create motion (convection).
- Viscous force resists this motion.
- The Grashoff number indicates whether buoyancy (natural convection) is strong enough to overcome viscous resistance.

B   Differentiate between:

1) Nusselt number and Reynolds number. 2) Free convection and forced convection.

Parameter	Nusselt Number (Nu)	Reynolds Number (Re)
Definition	Ratio of convective to conductive heat transfer across a boundary	Ratio of inertial forces to viscous forces in a fluid flow
Formula	$Nu = hL/k$	$Re = \rho uL/\mu = uL/\nu$
Significance	Measures effectiveness of convection relative to conduction	Determines the flow regime: laminar, transitional, or turbulent
Use in Heat Transfer	Used to calculate the convective heat transfer coefficient: h	Helps determine whether the flow is laminar or turbulent, affecting heat transfer and drag
Interpretation	- Nu = 1: pure conduction - Nu > 1: convection present	- Re < 2000: laminar - 2000 < Re < 4000: transitional - Re > 4000: turbulent
Application	Heat exchanger design, natural/forced convection analysis	Fluid flow analysis in pipes, ducts, and around objects

Aspect	Free Convection	Forced Convection
Definition	Fluid motion occurs due to buoyancy forces caused by temperature differences	Fluid motion is induced externally by fans, pumps, or blowers
Driving Force	Density differences in the fluid due to temperature gradients.	Mechanical devices provide the driving force.
Examples	- Air rising from a hot surface - Cooling of a hot cup of tea in still air	- Water flowing over a heated coil - Air blown by a fan over fins
Heat Transfer Rate	Generally lower	Typically, higher due to higher fluid velocity
Governing Dimensionless Numbers	- Grashoff Number (Gr) - Prandtl Number (Pr)	- Reynolds Number (Re) - Prandtl Number (Pr)
Flow Control	Not easily controlled; depends on fluid properties and geometry	Can be precisely controlled via flow rate adjustment
Design Complexity	Simpler systems (no moving parts)	Requires external equipment (fans, pumps), increasing complexity
Applications	- Electronics cooling in passive systems - Solar collectors	- Automotive radiators - Air conditioning systems - Heat exchangers

C   **Using Buckingham – π theorem show that Nusselt number for free convection is a function of Grashoff Number and Prandtl number.**

Solution : Here in case of free convection velocity V, which was responsible for flow in forced convection is replaced by variables β, g, Δt, because here the velocity of fluid is very slow and flow is caused due to density difference. Combined $\left(\beta g \Delta t\right)$ represents buoyancy parameter which is causing the flow, so we will consider it as a single quantity.

Considering M-L-T-θ-H system here. The dimensions of various quantities are :

Variable	Symbol	Dimension
Heat Transfer co-efficient	h	$HL^{-2}T^{-1}\theta^{-1}$
Co-efficient of thermal expansion	β	θ^{-1}
Gravitational Acceleration	g	LT^{-2}
Temperature Difference	ΔT	θ
Characteristic length	l	L
Fluid density	ρ	ML^{-3}
Fluid viscosity	μ	$ML^{-1}T^{-1}$
Fluid Thermal conductivity	k	$HL^{-1}T^{-1}\theta^{-1}$
Specific heat (heat capacity)	C_p	$HM^{-1}\theta^{-1}$

$\rightarrow$ **Buckingham's π Theorem :** Here the functional relationship given is :

$$h = f\left(\mu, \rho, k, C_p, \beta g \Delta t, l\right) = 0$$

or $\quad f'\left(h, \mu, \rho, k, C_p, \beta g \Delta t, l\right) = 0$

If we consider $\left(\beta g \Delta t\right)$ as combined quantity total quantities involved will be seven & no. of fundamental quantities used here as five. So no. of non-dimensional π group will be $(7-5) = 2$ only, which will not satisfy the required answer. (i.e. $Nu = \phi\left(Gr, Pr\right)$). Thus, we need to consider $\left(\beta g\right)$ and $\left(\Delta t\right)$ are two separate quantities for some cases. So now total quantities will be eight so ($\beta g \Delta t$) & thus no. of π-groups will be 3.

But in this case, no. of repeated variables will be 4, because, no flow property (V or g) is there. Selecting l (geometric), μ (fluid property), $\beta g \Delta t$ (temp. property), k (thermal property) as repeatating quantities, we get π_1-term.

$$\pi_1 = \mu^{a_1} k^{b_1} \left(\beta g \Delta t\right)^{c_1} (l)^{d_1} h \qquad \ldots(\text{I})$$

Putting dimensions for all, we get

$$M^o L^o T^o \theta^o H^o = \left[ML^{-1}T^{-1}\right]^{a_1} \left[HL^{-1}T^{-1}\theta^{-1}\right]^{b_1} \left[LT^{-2}\right]^{c_1} [L]^{d_1} \left[HL^{-2}T^{-1}\theta^{-1}\right]$$

Equating components for $M . L . T . \theta \ \& \ H$:

For M : 0 $= a_1$

  L : 0 $= -a_1 - b_1 + c_1 + d_1 - 2$

  T : 0 $= -a_1 - b_1 - 2c_1 - 1$

  θ : 0 $= -b_1 - 1$

  H : 0 $= b_1 + 1$

Equating above equations we get

$$a_1 = 0, \ b_1 = -1, \ c_1 = 0, \ d_1 = 1$$

Putting these values in equation (I)

$$\pi_1 = \frac{hl}{k}$$

π_2-**term :** $\pi_2 = \mu^{a_2} k^{b_2} \left(\beta g \Delta t \right)^{c_2} l^{d_2} \rho$

By doing same procedure we will get $\pi_2 = \dfrac{l^3 \rho^2 \left(\beta g \Delta t \right)}{\mu^2}$

π_3-**term :** $\pi_3 = \mu^{a_3} k^{b_3} \left(\beta g \Delta t \right)^{c_3} l^{d_3} C_p$

We will get $\pi_3 = \dfrac{\mu C_p}{k}$

Now, $\pi_1 = \phi \left(\pi_2, \pi_3 \right)$

$$\therefore \ \frac{hl}{k} = \phi \left(\frac{l^3 \rho^2 \left(\beta g \Delta t \right)}{\mu^2}, \ \frac{\mu C_p}{k} \right)$$

Thus, $Nu = \phi \left(Gr, Pr \right)$

or $\qquad Nu = C_1 Gr^{c_2} Pr^{c_3}$

where c_1, c_2, c_3 constants are found out by experiments.

Q.3 A) Describe mean film temperature and bulk mean temperature.

The mean film temperature is the average temperature between the surface and the surrounding fluid. Used to evaluate fluid properties (like viscosity, thermal conductivity, etc.) when calculating heat transfer coefficients in convection. The bulk mean temperature is the average temperature of the fluid flowing through a pipe or duct, weighted by mass flow rate or energy flow.

Used in calculating heat transfer between a flowing fluid and a surface, especially in forced convection.

Aspect	Mean Film Temperature (Tf)	Bulk Mean Temperature (Tm)
Used For	Evaluating fluid properties for calculations	Energy balance in flowing fluids
Based On	Surface and ambient temperatures	Cross-sectional average temperature of flowing fluid
Typical Application	Free and forced convection	Internal flows (pipes, ducts, channels)

B **Explain the concept of thermal boundary layers.**

When a fluid flows over a solid surface that is at a different temperature than the fluid, a thermal boundary layer is formed. This is a region in the fluid near the surface where the temperature changes from that of the surface to that of the free stream fluid. Heat transfer occurs between the surface and the fluid primarily within this layer due to conduction and convection.

The thermal boundary layer begins to form at the leading edge of the surface and grows in thickness along the direction of flow. Its thickness is typically defined as the distance from the surface to the point in the fluid where the temperature reaches 99% of the free stream value.

The thickness and behavior of the thermal boundary layer depend on the properties of the fluid, the velocity of the flow, and the temperature difference between the surface and the fluid. For fluids with a high Prandtl number (like oil), the thermal boundary layer is thinner than the velocity boundary layer. For fluids with a low Prandtl number (like liquid metals), the thermal boundary layer is thicker.

The thermal boundary layer is crucial in convective heat transfer analysis because the rate of heat transfer between the surface and the fluid is strongly influenced by the temperature gradient within this layer.

C **A horizontal fluorescent tube which is 3.8 cm in diameter and 120 cm long stands in still air at 1 bar and 20^{0}C. If the surface temperature is 40^{0}C and radiation is neglected, calculate heat transfer rate by convection.**
Use Nu = 0.53 (Gr.Pr)$^{0.25}$

From Air Table (Properties of Air) at T$_{mf}$
v =15.06 X 10-6 m^2/sec,
 Pr=0.701,
K= 2.673 X 10-2 W/mK

- Length of tube, $L = 120\,\text{cm} = 1.2\,\text{m}$
- Surface temperature, $T_s = 40^\circ C$
- Ambient temperature, $T_\infty = 20^\circ C$
- Air properties at mean film temperature $T_{mf} = \frac{T_s + T_\infty}{2} = \frac{40 + 20}{2} = 30^\circ C$
    - Kinematic viscosity, $\nu = 15.06 \times 10^{-6}\,\text{m}^2/\text{s}$
    - Prandtl number, $Pr = 0.701$
    - Thermal conductivity, $k = 2.673 \times 10^{-2}\,\text{W/mK}$
- Acceleration due to gravity, $g = 9.81\,\text{m/s}^2$
- Coefficient of thermal expansion, $\beta = \frac{1}{T_{mf} + 273} = \frac{1}{30 + 273} = \frac{1}{303}\,\text{K}^{-1}$

Step 1: Calculate temperature difference, ΔT

$$\Delta T = T_s - T_\infty = 40 - 20 = 20^\circ C$$

Step 2: Calculate Grashof number, Gr

$$Gr = \frac{g\,\beta\,\Delta T\,D^3}{\nu^2}$$

$$Gr = \frac{9.81 \times \frac{1}{303} \times 20 \times (0.038)^3}{(15.06 \times 10^{-6})^2}$$

Calculate numerator:

$$9.81 \times 0.0033 \times 20 \times 5.487 \times 10^{-5} = 9.81 \times 0.0033 \times 0.001097 = 3.55 \times 10^{-5}$$

Calculate denominator:

$$(15.06 \times 10^{-6})^2 = 2.27 \times 10^{-10}$$

Thus,

$$Gr = \frac{3.55 \times 10^{-5}}{2.27 \times 10^{-10}} = 1.56 \times 10^5$$

Step 3: Calculate Nusselt number, Nu

$$Nu = 0.53(Gr \times Pr)^{0.25}$$

$$Nu = 0.53 \times (1.56 \times 10^5 \times 0.701)^{0.25} = 0.53 \times (1.09 \times 10^5)^{0.25}$$

Calculate:

$$(1.09 \times 10^5)^{0.25} = (10^{5.04})^{0.25} = 10^{1.26} = 18.2$$

Therefore,

$$Nu = 0.53 \times 18.2 = 9.65$$

Step 4: Calculate heat transfer coefficient, h

$$h = \frac{Nu \times k}{D} = \frac{9.65 \times 0.02673}{0.038} = \frac{0.2578}{0.038} = 6.79\,\text{W/m}^2\text{K}$$

Step 5: Calculate surface area, A

$$A = \pi D L = \pi \times 0.038 \times 1.2 = 0.1432\,\text{m}^2$$

Step 6: Calculate heat transfer rate, Q

$$Q = h \times A \times \Delta T = 6.79 \times 0.1432 \times 20 = 19.44 \text{ W}$$

Final answer:

$$\boxed{Q = 19.44 \text{ W}}$$

This is the heat transfer rate by natural convection from the horizontal fluorescent tube.

Q.4 A) Define absorptivity, emissivity and monochromatic emissive power.

Absorptivity: Absorptivity is the fraction of the incident radiation that a surface absorbs. It is a dimensionless quantity ranging from 0 to 1.

Emissivity: Emissivity is the ratio of the radiation emitted by a surface to the radiation emitted by a blackbody at the same temperature. It is a measure of how effectively a surface emits thermal radiation compared to a perfect emitter (blackbody).

Monochromatic Emissive Power: Monochromatic emissive power is the amount of radiant energy emitted by a surface per unit area per unit wavelength at a particular wavelength λ.

B   Describe shape factor. Discuss salient features of shape factor.

Shape Factor (View Factor or Configuration Factor)

The shape factor (also called view factor or configuration factor) between two surfaces is the fraction of the radiation leaving one surface that directly reaches and is intercepted by the other surface.

It is denoted by F1→2.

 It depends only on geometry, not on material properties or temperatures.

Salient Features of Shape Factor

1. Reciprocity Rule:
      A1F1→2=A2F2→1
   This relates the view factors between two surfaces.
2. Self-View Factor:
   o   For flat or convex surfaces, Fi→i=0 (they do not see themselves).
   o   For concave surfaces, Fi→i≠0.
3. Depends on Geometry:
   o   Shape factors are purely geometric and are independent of temperature or surface properties.
4. Used in Radiation Heat Transfer:
   o   Essential in calculating radiative exchange between surfaces in enclosures.
5. Symmetry in Shape Factor:
   o   Often used to simplify calculations in symmetrical geometries like parallel plates, concentric cylinders, or spheres.

C   Define total emissive power (Eb) and intensity of radiation (Ib). Show that Eb = $\pi \times$Ib

Monochromatic or spectral intensity of radiation is defined as the radiant energy emitted by a black body at a temperature T, streaming through an unit area normal to the direction of propagation, per unit wavelength about a wavelength, per unit solid angle about the propagation of beam. It is denoted by $I_{b\lambda}$ and can be expressed as :

$$I_{b\lambda} = \frac{\text{Energy emitted}}{(\text{Projected area}) \times (\text{Wave length}) \times (\text{Solid angle})}; \frac{W}{m^2 \cdot \mu m \cdot Sr} \quad ...(23)$$

$$\therefore \text{Radiation intensity } (I_b) = \int_{\lambda=0}^{\lambda=\alpha} I_{b\lambda} \cdot d\lambda; \ W/m^2 \cdot Sr \quad ...(24)$$

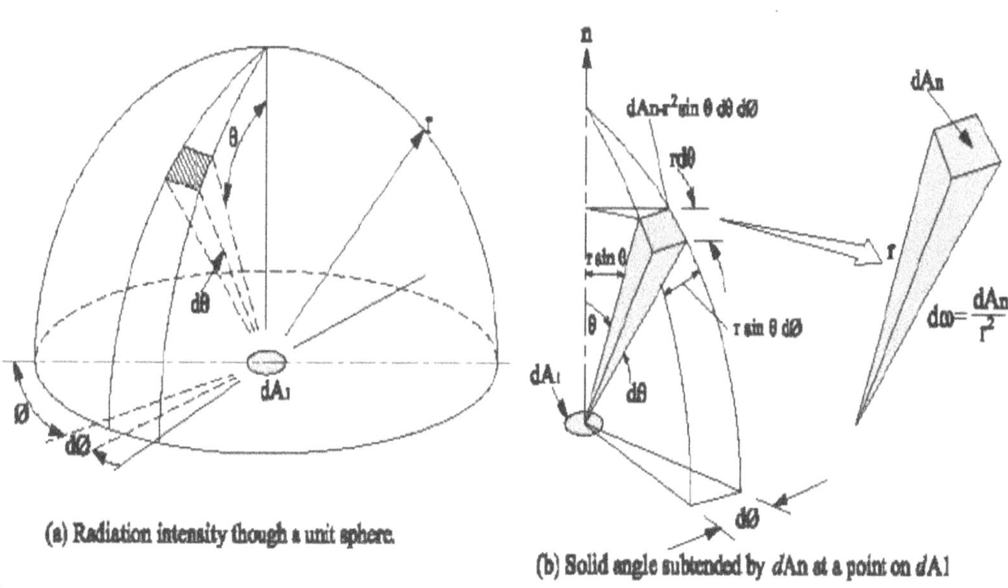

(a) Radiation intensity though a unit sphere.

(b) Solid angle subtended by dAn at a point on $dA1$

Figure 7 : Radiation intensity

The radiation intensity (I_b) may be defined as the radiation energy emitted by a black body at temperature T over all wavelength per unit solid angle and per unit area.

Refer figure no. 7. Consider radiant energy emitted from the centre of hemisphere with elemental area dAl. Let this emission is absorbed by a portion of hemisphere (elemental area $= dAn$). The area dAn makes an angle $d\theta$ with dA_1 by joining perpendicular line.

$\therefore$ The solid angle subtended by dAn,

$$d\omega = \frac{dAn}{r^2}$$

where, $\quad d\omega = \sin\theta \cdot d\theta \cdot d\phi$

Also from figure 7(b), we say

$$dAn = r^2 \cdot \sin\theta \cdot d\theta \cdot d\phi \qquad \qquad ...(i)$$

and monochromatic intensity of radiation $\left(I_{b\lambda}\right)$

$$I_{b\lambda} = \frac{dQ_\lambda}{d_{A1} \cdot \cos\theta \cdot \dfrac{dAn}{r^2}} \qquad \qquad ...(ii)$$

By rearranging equation (ii) and using equation (i), we have

$$dQ_\lambda = I_{b\lambda} \cdot \sin\theta \cdot \cos\theta \cdot dA_1 \cdot d\theta \cdot d\phi$$

The monochromatic emissive power associated with d_{A1} is

$$dE_\lambda = \frac{dQ_\lambda}{dA_1} = I_{b\lambda} \cdot \cos\theta \cdot \sin\theta \cdot d\phi \cdot d\theta \qquad \qquad ...(iii)$$

For the known value of $I_{b\lambda}$, $E_{b\lambda}$ is function of θ and ϕ of the hemisphere.

Maximum values of ϕ and θ are,

$$\phi = 2\pi, \ \theta = \frac{\pi}{2}$$

$$\therefore E_{b\lambda} = \int_{\phi=0}^{\phi=2\pi} \int_{\phi=0}^{\theta=\pi/2} I_{b\lambda} \cdot \cos\theta \cdot \sin\theta \cdot d\phi \cdot d\theta \qquad \qquad ...(iv)$$

and the total emissive power of black body (E) is

$$E_b = \int_{\lambda=0}^{\lambda=\infty} E_{b\lambda} \cdot d\lambda \qquad \qquad ...(v)$$

For the diffused radiation, intensity of radiation is independent of direction. So,

$$E_{b\lambda} = I_{b\lambda} \cdot \int_0^{2\pi} \int_0^{\pi/2} \cos\theta \cdot \sin\theta \cdot d\phi \cdot d\theta \qquad \qquad ...(vi)$$

$$\therefore E_{b\lambda} = \pi \cdot I_{b\lambda} \cdot \int_0^{\pi/2} \sin\theta \cdot d\theta$$

$$\therefore E_{b\lambda}(T) = \pi \cdot I_{b\lambda}(T)$$

where, T = temperature of the surface ; k

So, $\quad E_b = \pi \cdot I_b \qquad \qquad ...(25)$

Q.4 **A) It is desirable to wear white clothes instead of black during the summer season. Give reason.**

It is desirable to wear white clothes instead of black during the summer season because of the way different colors interact with sunlight:

- White clothes reflect most of the sunlight (including the visible spectrum and a portion of infrared radiation). This reflection helps in minimizing the absorption of heat, keeping the body cooler.
- Black clothes absorb most of the sunlight, including heat energy, which leads to greater heat absorption and makes the body feel hotter.

Wearing white or light-colored clothes during summer helps keep the body cooler by reflecting sunlight, while black or dark-colored clothes make you feel hotter by absorbing more heat.

B **Draw temperature variation for condenser and evaporator of thermal power plant.**

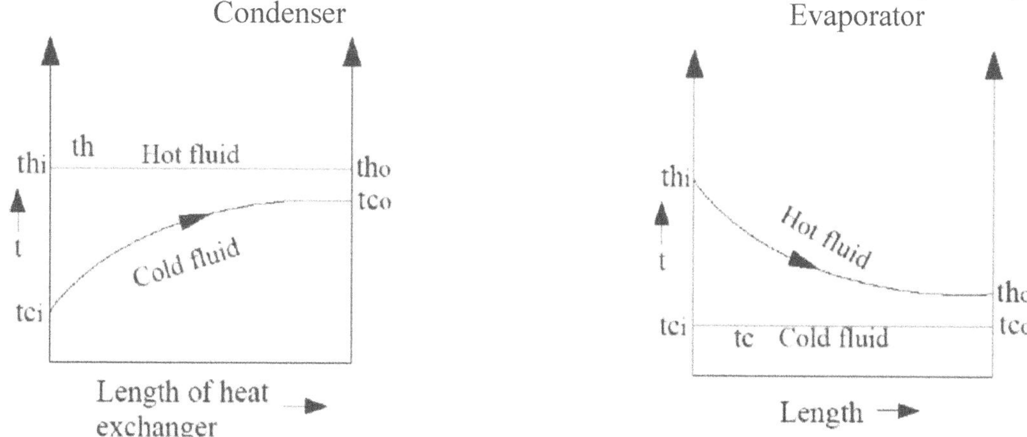

C **Two large parallel plates with $\epsilon = 0.4$ each are maintained at different temperatures and are exchanging heat only by radiation. Two equally large radiation shields with surface emissivity 0.04 are introduced in parallel to the plates. Find the percentage reduction in net radiation heat transfer.**

Given:

Emissivity of each plate, $\varepsilon_1 = \varepsilon_2 = 0.4$

Emissivity of each shield, $\varepsilon_s = 0.04$

Number of shields = 2

Step 1: Heat transfer without shield

The net radiative heat transfer between two large parallel plates is given by:

$$q_{\text{no shield}} = \frac{\sigma(T_1^4 - T_2^4)}{\left(\frac{1}{\varepsilon_1} + \frac{1}{\varepsilon_2} - 1\right)}$$

Substituting $\varepsilon_1 = \varepsilon_2 = 0.4$:

$$q_{\text{no shield}} = \frac{\sigma(T_1^4 - T_2^4)}{\left(\frac{1}{0.4} + \frac{1}{0.4} - 1\right)} = \frac{\sigma(T_1^4 - T_2^4)}{5}$$

Step 2: Heat transfer with two shields

When two radiation shields are inserted, the thermal resistance is the sum of resistances between each surface:

$$R = \left(\frac{1}{\varepsilon_1} - 1\right) + \left(\frac{2}{\varepsilon_s} - 2\right) + \left(\frac{1}{\varepsilon_2} - 1\right)$$

$$R = \left(\frac{1}{0.4} - 1\right) + \left(\frac{2}{0.04} - 2\right) + \left(\frac{1}{0.4} - 1\right) = 1.5 + 48 + 1.5 = 51$$

So, the heat transfer with shields:

$$q_{\text{with shields}} = \frac{\sigma(T_1^4 - T_2^4)}{51}$$

Step 3: Percentage reduction in heat transfer:

$$\text{Percentage reduction} = \left(\frac{q_{\text{no shield}} - q_{\text{with shields}}}{q_{\text{no shield}}}\right) \times 100$$

$$= \left(\frac{\frac{1}{5} - \frac{1}{51}}{\frac{1}{5}}\right) \times 100 = \left(1 - \frac{1/51}{1/5}\right) \times 100 = \left(1 - \frac{5}{51}\right) \times 100 = \left(\frac{46}{51}\right) \times 100 \approx 90.2\%$$

Q.5 **A) Justify that a good absorber is also a good emitter for radiation heat transfer.**

According to Kirchhoff's Law of Thermal Radiation, at thermal equilibrium, the emissivity (ε) of a surface is equal to its absorptivity (α\alpha$\alpha$) at every wavelength and temperature:

$\varepsilon = \alpha$. This means a material that absorbs a high fraction of incident radiation (i.e., a good absorber) must also emit radiation efficiently (i.e., be a good emitter).

Explanation:

- When a body is at a given temperature, it emits radiation based on its temperature and surface properties.
- If a body were a good absorber but poor emitter, it would gain more energy than it loses, contradicting the second law of thermodynamics.
- For thermal equilibrium, the rate of absorption must equal the rate of emission.
- Therefore, a surface that absorbs most radiation it receives also emits most of the energy it can.

B **Give broad classification of heat exchangers.**

Heat exchangers are devices used to transfer heat between two or more fluids at different temperatures. They are widely used in industries such as power generation, chemical processing, refrigeration, and HVAC systems. Heat exchangers can be broadly classified based on various criteria, as described below:

1. Based on the Nature of Heat Exchange Process:

- Direct Contact Heat Exchangers: In these heat exchangers, the two fluids come into direct physical contact and exchange heat. They are typically used when mixing of fluids is permissible. Examples include cooling towers and jet condensers.
- Indirect Contact Heat Exchangers: In this type, the fluids do not mix and are separated by a solid wall. Heat is transferred through conduction and convection across the wall. These are the most common types in industrial applications.

2. Based on Relative Direction of Fluid Flow:
- Parallel Flow Heat Exchangers: Both the hot and cold fluids enter the exchanger at the same end and move in the same direction. This configuration is simple but less efficient in terms of temperature change.
- Counter Flow Heat Exchangers: The fluids enter the exchanger from opposite ends and flow in opposite directions. This arrangement provides the highest efficiency and greater temperature difference between fluids.
- Cross Flow Heat Exchangers: The two fluids flow perpendicular to each other. These are commonly used in air-cooled applications such as automobile radiators.

3. Based on Design and Construction:
- Shell and Tube Heat Exchangers: Composed of a series of tubes enclosed in a cylindrical shell. One fluid flow through the tubes, while the other flows outside the tubes within the shell. They are widely used in oil refineries and power plants.
- Plate Heat Exchangers: Made up of multiple thin metal plates with large surface areas, stacked together to form channels for fluid flow. They provide high heat transfer efficiency and are used in food processing and chemical industries.
- Finned Tube Heat Exchangers: Incorporate fins on the tubes to increase the surface area and improve heat transfer, especially in air-side heat transfer applications.
- Double Pipe Heat Exchangers: Consist of one pipe inside another, allowing one fluid to flow through the inner pipe and another fluid through the annular space between the pipes. Suitable for small-scale applications.

4. Based on Number of Fluids:
- Two-Fluid Heat Exchangers: Involve the exchange of heat between two fluids. This is the most common configuration.
- Multi-Fluid Heat Exchangers: Designed to handle more than two fluids, often used in complex systems such as combined cycle power plants or chemical reactors.

5. Based on Transfer Process Configuration:
- Recuperative Heat Exchangers: The fluids flow on either side of a solid heat transfer surface without mixing. Heat is transferred directly through the separating wall. Examples include shell and tube and plate heat exchangers.
- Regenerative Heat Exchangers: A single medium, usually a matrix or a rotating wheel, alternately stores heat from the hot fluid and transfers it to the cold fluid. These are typically used in gas turbines and air preheaters.

Derive the equation of LMTD for counter-flow heat exchangers.

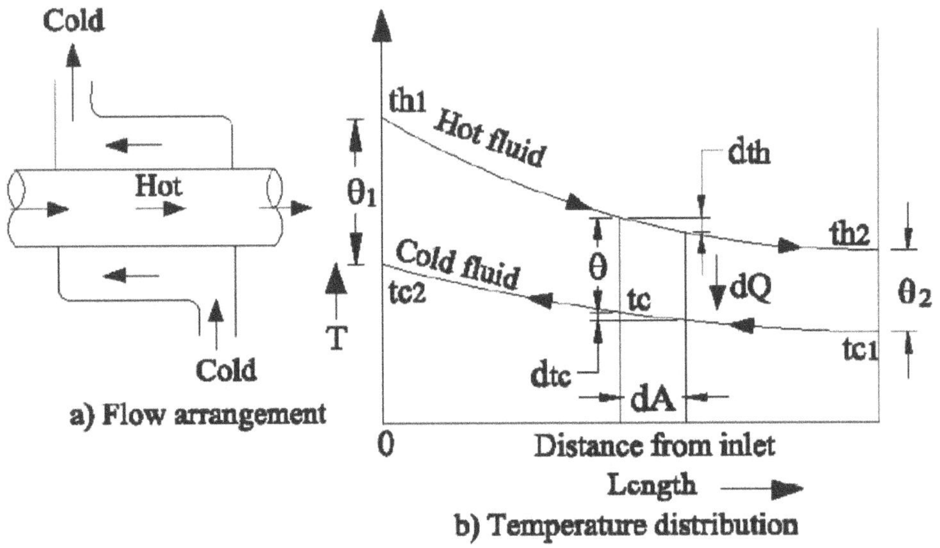

Figure 13 : Counter flow heat exchanger

Let us consider an elementary area dA of the heat exchanger. The rate of flow of heat through this elementary area is given by (Refer figure no. 13)

$$dQ = U \cdot dA \left(t_h - t_c \right) = U \cdot dA \cdot \Delta t$$

In this case also, the heat balance over a differential area dA may be written as

$$dQ = -\dot{m}_c \cdot c_{pc} \cdot dt_c = -\dot{m}_h \cdot c_{ph} \cdot dt_h$$

In a counter-flow system, the temperatures of both the fluids decrease in the direction of heat exchanger length, hence the negative signs.

$$\therefore dt_h = -\frac{dQ}{\dot{m}_h c_{ph}} = -\frac{dQ}{C_h}$$

and,
$$dt_c = -\frac{dQ}{\dot{m}_h c_{pc}} = -\frac{dQ}{C_c}$$

$$\therefore dt_h - dt_c = -dQ \left[\frac{1}{C_h} - \frac{1}{C_c} \right]$$

and
$$d\theta = -dQ \left[\frac{1}{C_h} - \frac{1}{C_c} \right] \qquad ...(11)$$

Inserting the value of dQ, we get

$$d\theta = -U \, dA \left(t_h - t_c \right) \left[\frac{1}{C_h} - \frac{1}{C_c} \right]$$

$$\therefore d\theta = -U \, dA \cdot \theta \left[\frac{1}{C_h} - \frac{1}{C_c} \right]$$

So,
$$\frac{d\theta}{\theta} = -U\,dA \cdot \left[\frac{1}{C_h} - \frac{1}{C_c}\right]$$

Integrating the above equation from $A = 0$ to $A = A$, we get

$$\ln\left(\theta_2 / \theta_1\right) = -U.A\left[\frac{1}{C_h} - \frac{1}{C_c}\right]$$

Now, the total heat transfer rate between the two fluids is given by

$$Q = C_h\left(t_{h1} - t_{h2}\right) = C_c\left(t_{c2} - t_{c1}\right)$$

So,
$$\frac{1}{C_h} = \frac{t_{h1} - t_{h2}}{Q}$$

and
$$\frac{1}{C_c} = \frac{t_{c2} - t_{c1}}{Q}$$

substituting the values of $\dfrac{1}{C_h}$ and $\dfrac{1}{C_c}$ in equation (12), we have,

$$\ln\left(\theta_2 / \theta_1\right) = -U\,A\left[\frac{t_{h1} - t_{h2}}{Q} - \frac{t_{c2} - t_{c1}}{Q}\right]$$

$$= -\frac{UA}{Q}\left[\left(t_{h1} - t_{c2}\right) - \left(t_{h2} - t_{c1}\right)\right] = -\frac{UA}{Q}\left(\theta_1 - \theta_2\right) = \frac{UA}{Q}\left(\theta_2 - \theta_1\right)$$

or
$$Q = \frac{UA\left(\theta_2 - \theta_1\right)}{\ln\left(\theta_2 / \theta_1\right)}$$

Since, $\quad Q = U\,A\,\theta_m$

Q.5 A) Define fouling factor in case of heat exchanger? List the causes of fouling.

The fouling factor (Rf) is a measure of the resistance to heat transfer caused by the accumulation of unwanted materials (fouling) on the heat transfer surfaces of a heat exchanger. It is defined as the thermal resistance per unit area due to the fouling layer.

Causes of Fouling

1. Scaling: Deposition of dissolved minerals like calcium carbonate from hard water forming a hard scale layer.
2. Corrosion Products: Formation of rust or other corrosion by-products that accumulate on surfaces.
3. Biological Growth: Growth of microorganisms such as algae, bacteria, and fungi (biofouling).
4. Particulate Fouling: Deposition of suspended solids or dirt particles carried by the fluid.
5. Chemical Reaction Fouling: Formation of deposits due to chemical reactions between the fluid and surface or within the fluid.
6. Mud and Sludge: Accumulation of sludge or mud in fluids containing impurities.

B **Discuss the various regimes of boiling.**

Boiling is a complex heat transfer process that occurs when a liquid is heated to its saturation temperature and undergoes a phase change to vapor. The boiling process can be classified into different regimes depending on the surface temperature and heat flux. These regimes are generally represented by the boiling curve, which plots heat flux against the temperature difference between the heating surface and the liquid saturation temperature.

The various regimes of boiling are as follows:

1. Natural Convection Boiling (Interfacial Evaporation): This occurs at low surface temperatures, just above the saturation temperature of the liquid. The heat transfer takes place primarily by natural convection. A small amount of vapor may form at isolated nucleation sites, but bulk boiling does not occur.

2. Nucleate Boiling: As the surface temperature increases further, vapor bubbles begin to form at nucleation sites on the heating surface. These bubbles grow and detach from the surface, rising into the liquid. This regime is highly efficient in transferring heat.

3. Critical Heat Flux (CHF) or Departure from Nucleate Boiling (DNB): At this point, the heat flux reaches its maximum value. Beyond this point, the formation of vapor blankets begins to interfere with heat transfer. It marks the transition from nucleate boiling to film boiling.

4. Transition Boiling: This is an unstable regime between nucleate and film boiling. The surface is partially covered with vapor, leading to fluctuating heat transfer. The vapor film is intermittently disrupted, exposing the surface to liquid and causing temperature spikes.

5. Film Boiling: At very high surface temperatures, the surface becomes completely covered with a stable vapor film that insulates it from the liquid. Heat is transferred mainly through conduction and radiation across the vapor layer.

Understanding the various regimes of boiling is critical in the design of boilers, nuclear reactors, and other thermal systems to ensure efficient heat transfer and avoid surface damage due to excessive temperatures.

C **Define condensation? Explain film-wise condensation and drop-wise condensation.**

Condensation is the process by which a vapor changes into its liquid phase when it comes in contact with a surface at a temperature below the vapor's saturation temperature.

Types of Condensation

1. Film-wise Condensation: In film-wise condensation, the condensed liquid forms a continuous thin film over the cooling surface. This film grows thicker as condensation proceeds and offers resistance to heat transfer because heat must conduct through the liquid film to the surface.

Characteristics:

- Occurs on surfaces that are wettable by the liquid.
- Heat transfer coefficient is generally lower due to the insulating effect of the liquid film.

Example: Condensation on the outside of a cold pipe or a vertical tube in power plants where water vapor condenses forming a continuous water film.

2. Drop-wise Condensation: In drop-wise condensation, the condensate forms discrete droplets on the surface instead of a continuous film. These droplets coalesce and fall off the surface, exposing fresh surface area to vapor, which enhances heat transfer.

Characteristics:
- Occurs on non-wettable or hydrophobic surfaces.
- Heat transfer rates can be 5 to 7 times higher than film-wise condensation.

Example:

Condensation on a freshly waxed car windshield or on specially treated condenser tubes with hydrophobic coatings.

PAPER 5_ 3151909: HEAT TRANSFER

WINTER 2020 EXAM   DATE: 27/01/2021

Q.1 A) Explain aims to study 'Heat Transfer'?

The primary aim of studying heat transfer in mechanical engineering is to understand how thermal energy moves within and between materials.

This knowledge helps engineers design systems like engines, heat exchangers, and cooling units more efficiently. It also supports energy conservation, enhances system performance, and ensures safety in thermal applications.

Mastery of heat transfer principles is essential for solving practical engineering problems related to heating, cooling, and energy use.

B Differentiate between: 1) Conduction and radiation. 2) Counter-flow and parallel flow heat exchanger.

Conduction	Radiation
Transfer of heat through a solid or between solids in direct contact.	Transfer of heat through electromagnetic waves without the need for a medium.
Requires a material medium (usually solids).	Does not require any medium; can occur in a vacuum.
Occurs due to the collision and vibration of particles.	Occurs via electromagnetic waves, typically infrared.
Heat transfer from a stove to a metal pot.	Heat from the Sun reaching the Earth.
Generally slower, depends on the material's conductivity.	Very fast; travels at the speed of light.

Counter-Flow Heat Exchanger	Parallel Flow Heat Exchanger
Fluids flow in opposite directions.	Both fluids flow in the same direction.
Maintains a higher temperature difference along the length, improving efficiency.	Temperature difference decreases quickly along the flow path.
More efficient due to larger average temperature difference.	Less efficient compared to counter-flow design.
Cold fluid can be heated to a temperature close to the hot fluid's inlet temperature.	Cold fluid cannot reach the inlet temperature of the hot fluid.
Used in applications requiring high heat transfer efficiency, such as condensers and boilers.	Used where simplicity is more important than efficiency.

C What is meant by thermal resistance? Explain the electrical analogy for solving heat transfer problems.

Thermal resistance is a measure of a material's ability to resist the flow of heat. It represents how much a material or system opposes the transfer of thermal energy when there is a temperature difference across it.

The higher the thermal resistance, the less heat is transferred.

It is commonly used in heat transfer analysis, especially in conduction, and is analogous to electrical resistance in an electric circuit.

We know that due to voltage difference, current can flow through electrical circuit and the system offer some resistance to the flow of current.

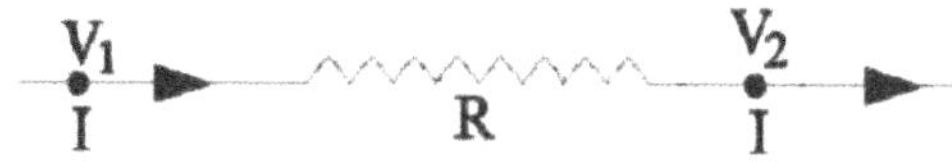

Figure 3 : Electrical circuit

where, $V_1 - V_2$ = voltage difference,

I = current flow.

R = Resistance offered by system to flow of current

According to Ohm's law,

$$V = IR$$

$$\therefore \frac{V_1 - V_2}{R} = I \qquad \qquad ...(6)$$

In case of thermal engineering, due to temperature difference heat will flow through the system/plane wall or slab and it offers the resistance to the flow of heat. That resistance is known as thermal resistance. The thermal circuit is shown in figure 4.

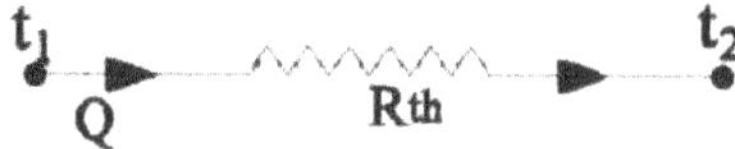

Figure 4 : Thermal circuit

where, $t_1 - t_2$ = temperature difference,

Q = heat flow

R_{th} = thermal Resistance offered by the material

$$\therefore \Delta t = R_{th} \cdot Q$$

$$\therefore \frac{t_1 - t_2}{R_{th}} = Q \qquad \qquad ...(6a)$$

By equating equations (6a) and (5), we get

$$R_{th} = \frac{L}{AK} = \text{thermal resistance offered in case of plane wall/slab} \qquad ...(7)$$

Q.2 A) Use of aluminum material as a cooking utensil are not desirable. Evaluate.

Aluminium is widely used in cookware due to its excellent thermal conductivity, light weight, and low cost. However, there are several concerns that make its use in cooking utensils less desirable in certain situations:

1. Reactivity with Food: Aluminium is a highly reactive metal. It can react with acidic or salty foods, such as tomatoes or vinegar-based dishes, leading to a metallic taste and potential leaching of aluminium into the food. This may raise health concerns over long-term exposure.

2. Health Concerns: Although scientific studies have not conclusively proven that aluminium causes health issues like Alzheimer's disease, the possibility of aluminium accumulation in the body has raised public concern. This has led many to avoid uncoated aluminium cookware.

3. Durability: Aluminium is a soft metal and can easily warp or scratch. When scratched, more aluminium is exposed to food, increasing the chances of chemical interaction.

4. Staining and Discoloration: Aluminium cookware often stains and discolors with time, especially when used with certain ingredients or under high heat, affecting its appearance and sometimes its functionality.

While aluminum has advantages in terms of heat transfer and cost, its direct use in cooking utensils can be undesirable due to chemical reactivity and health concerns.

B   Give broad classification of heat exchangers.

Heat exchangers are devices used to transfer heat between two or more fluids at different temperatures. They are widely used in industries such as power generation, chemical processing, refrigeration, and HVAC systems. Heat exchangers can be broadly classified based on various criteria, as described below:

1. Based on the Nature of Heat Exchange Process:

- Direct Contact Heat Exchangers: In these heat exchangers, the two fluids come into direct physical contact and exchange heat. They are typically used when mixing of fluids is permissible. Examples include cooling towers and jet condensers.
- Indirect Contact Heat Exchangers: In this type, the fluids do not mix and are separated by a solid wall. Heat is transferred through conduction and convection across the wall. These are the most common types in industrial applications.

2. Based on Relative Direction of Fluid Flow:

- Parallel Flow Heat Exchangers: Both the hot and cold fluids enter the exchanger at the same end and move in the same direction. This configuration is simple but less efficient in terms of temperature change.
- Counter Flow Heat Exchangers: The fluids enter the exchanger from opposite ends and flow in opposite directions. This arrangement provides the highest efficiency and greater temperature difference between fluids.
- Cross Flow Heat Exchangers: The two fluids flow perpendicular to each other. These are commonly used in air-cooled applications such as automobile radiators.

3. Based on Design and Construction:

- Shell and Tube Heat Exchangers: Composed of a series of tubes enclosed in a cylindrical shell. One fluid flow through the tubes, while the other flows outside the tubes within the shell. They are widely used in oil refineries and power plants.
- Plate Heat Exchangers: Made up of multiple thin metal plates with large surface areas, stacked together to form channels for fluid flow. They provide high heat transfer efficiency and are used in food processing and chemical industries.
- Finned Tube Heat Exchangers: Incorporate fins on the tubes to increase the surface area and improve heat transfer, especially in air-side heat transfer applications.
- Double Pipe Heat Exchangers: Consist of one pipe inside another, allowing one fluid to flow through the inner pipe and another fluid through the annular space between the pipes. Suitable for small-scale applications.

4. Based on Number of Fluids:
- Two-Fluid Heat Exchangers: Involve the exchange of heat between two fluids. This is the most common configuration.
- Multi-Fluid Heat Exchangers: Designed to handle more than two fluids, often used in complex systems such as combined cycle power plants or chemical reactors.

5. Based on Heat Transfer Mechanism:
- Single Phase Heat Exchangers: Both fluids remain in the same phase (either liquid or gas) throughout the heat exchange process. No phase change occurs.
- Two-Phase Heat Exchangers: At least one fluid undergoes a phase change, such as condensation or evaporation. These are used in boilers, condensers, and evaporators.

6. Based on Transfer Process Configuration:
- Recuperative Heat Exchangers: The fluids flow on either side of a solid heat transfer surface without mixing. Heat is transferred directly through the separating wall. Examples include shell and tube and plate heat exchangers.

Regenerative Heat Exchangers: A single medium, usually a matrix or a rotating wheel, alternately stores heat from the hot fluid and transfers it to the cold fluid. These are typically used in gas turbines and air preheaters.

C Write the most general equation in Cartesian co-ordinates for heat transfer by conduction. Deduce above equation for the following cases with suitable assumptions; (i) Laplace equation, (ii) Poisson equation, and (iii) Fourier equation.

$$\frac{\partial}{\partial x}\left(k_x \frac{\partial t}{\partial x}\right) + \frac{\partial}{\partial y}\left(k_y \frac{\partial t}{\partial y}\right) + \frac{\partial}{\partial z}\left(k_z \frac{\partial t}{\partial z}\right) + \dot{q}_g = \rho.c.\frac{\partial t}{\partial \tau} \qquad ...(14)$$

or, using the **vector operator** ∇, we get

$$\nabla.(k\nabla t) + \dot{q}_g = \rho.c.\frac{\partial t}{\partial \tau} \qquad ...(15)$$

This is known as the general heat conduction equation for 'non-homogeneous anisotropic material', 'Self heat generating' and 'unsteady three-dimensional heat flow.'

Case (i) When no internal source of heat generation is present. Eqn. (15-a) reduces to

$$\frac{\partial^2 t}{\partial x^2} + \frac{\partial^2 t}{\partial y^2} + \frac{\partial^2 t}{\partial z^2} = \frac{1}{\alpha}.\frac{\partial t}{\partial \tau} \qquad ...(17)$$

or, using Laplacian ∇^2,

$$\nabla^2 t = \frac{1}{\alpha}.\frac{\partial t}{\partial \tau} \quad \text{(Fourier's equation)} \qquad ...(18)$$

Case (ii) When the conduction then takes place in the steady state $\left(i.e. \dfrac{\partial t}{\partial \tau} = 0 \right)$, the equation (15-a) reduces to,

$$\frac{\partial^2 t}{\partial x^2} + \frac{\partial^2 t}{\partial y^2} + \frac{\partial^2 t}{\partial z^2} + \frac{\dot{q}_g}{k} = 0 \qquad \qquad ...(19)$$

$$\nabla^2 t + \frac{\dot{q}_g}{k} = 0 \ \text{(Poisson's equation)} \qquad \qquad ...(20)$$

In the absence of internal heat generation, Eqn. (20) reduces to

$$\frac{\partial^2 t}{\partial x^2} + \frac{\partial^2 t}{\partial y^2} + \frac{\partial^2 t}{\partial z^2} = 0 \qquad \qquad ...(21)$$

or, $\quad \nabla^2 t = 0$ (Laplace equation) $\qquad \qquad ...(22)$

OR

C   **Explain physical significance of critical radius of insulation and derive an expression for the same critical radius in case of sphere.**

Consider a hollow sphere of outer radius r_1 is covered with a layer of insulation with outer radius r_2 having constant thermal conductivity k. The sphere is exposed to environment where air is at temperature of t_{air} and h_{air} is convection heat transfer coefficient for air. $\left(h_o = h_{air} \right)$. Refer figure 19.

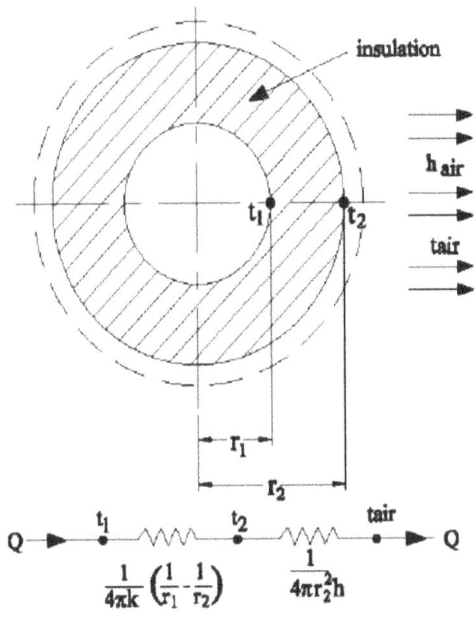

Figure 19 : Sphere with insulation

The heat flow rate can be expressed as :

$$Q = \frac{(t_1 - t_{air})}{\dfrac{1}{4\pi k}\left(\dfrac{1}{r_1} - \dfrac{1}{r_2}\right) + \dfrac{1}{4\pi r_2^2 \cdot h}}$$

Adopting the same procedure as that of a cylinder, we have

$$\frac{dQ}{dr_2} = 0$$

$$\therefore \frac{d}{dr_2}\left[\frac{1}{4\pi k}\left(\frac{1}{r_1} - \frac{1}{r_2}\right) + \frac{1}{4\pi r_2^2 \cdot h_o}\right] = 0$$

$$\therefore \frac{1}{k \cdot r_2^2} - \frac{2}{r_2^3 \cdot h_o} = 0$$

$$\therefore r_2 = r_c = \text{critical radius of sphere} = \frac{2k}{h_o}$$

Q.3 A) **In cold regions, instead of using one thick glass, two thin window glasses are preferred. Justify.**

In cold regions, using two thin glass panes with an air gap between them, commonly known as double glazing, is preferred over a single thick glass pane for the following reasons:

1. Better Insulation: The air gap between the two glass panes acts as an insulating layer. Air is a poor conductor of heat, so this trapped air reduces heat transfer by conduction, keeping indoor spaces warmer.
2. Reduced Heat Loss: A single thick glass pane conducts heat more readily compared to two thin panes separated by air. Double glazing reduces heat loss through the window significantly, improving energy efficiency.
3. Minimized Convection: The air gap limits air movement (convection) between the panes, further reducing heat loss.
4. Cost and Weight: Two thin panes are generally lighter and easier to manufacture and install than a single thick glass of equivalent thermal resistance.
5. Improved Comfort: Double glazing helps maintain a more consistent indoor temperature, reducing cold drafts near windows and increasing overall comfort.

B **Differentiate between: 1) Nusselt number and Reynolds number.**
2) Free convection and forced convection.

Nusselt Number (Nu)	Reynolds Number (Re)
A dimensionless number representing the ratio of convective to conductive heat transfer across a boundary.	A dimensionless number representing the ratio of inertial forces to viscous forces in a fluid flow.
Measures the enhancement of heat transfer through convection relative to conduction.	Determines the flow regime (laminar or turbulent) in fluid flow.
Useful for the Heat transfer analysis.	Useful for the Fluid flow dynamics.

Free Convection	Forced Convection
Heat transfers due to natural fluid motion caused by buoyancy forces from density differences.	Heat transfers due to fluid motion induced by external means like fans or pumps.
Temperature-induced density variations causing natural circulation.	External devices create fluid flow.
Generally slower and less controlled.	Typically, faster and controllable.
Warm air rising near a heater.	Air forced over a hot surface by a fan.
Usually, lower compared to forced convection.	Usually, higher due to increased fluid velocity.

C A cylinder in vertical position is having dimension of 18 cm diameter and length 1.5m is maintained at a temperature of 100^0C. It is kept in atmosphere having temperature 20^0C. Calculate the heat lost by cylinder surface to the atmosphere by free convection.

Properties of air at mean film temperature 60^0C are as follows:

ρ=1.06kg/m^3, υ=18.97*10^{-6}m^2/s,

k=0.1042kJ/m.hr.^{0}C, Cp=1.004kJ/kg^{0}C.

Use the relation Nu=0.10(Gr.Pr)$^{1/3}$

(The symbols have their usual meanings)

Solution :

Given data : $L = 1.5m$, $D = 18cm = 0.18m$, $t_s = 100°C$, $t_\infty = 20°C$, $\rho = 1.06 kg / m^3$,

$$\upsilon = 18.97 \times 10^{-6} m^2 / s, \; C_p = 1.004 kJ / kg°C = 1004 J / kg°C,$$

$$k = 0.1042 \, kJ / mh°C = \frac{0.1042 \times 10^3}{3600} \frac{W}{m°C} = 0.0289 \frac{W}{m\,°C}$$

$$t_{mf} = \frac{t_s + t_\infty}{2} = \frac{100 + 20}{2} = 60°C$$

Here characteristic length L_c is Length L of the cylinder

Heat loss by free convection Q :

$$\mu = \rho\upsilon = 1.06 \times \left(18.97 \times 10^{-6} \times 3600\right) = 0.07239 \, kg / m\,i$$

$$= \frac{0.07239}{3600} = 2 \times 10^{-5} \frac{kg}{m-s}$$

$$\beta = \frac{1}{T} = \frac{1}{273 + t_{mf}} = \frac{1}{273 + \left(\dfrac{100 + 20}{2}\right)} = 0.003 K^{-1}$$

$$Gr = \frac{\beta g \Delta t L^3 \rho^2}{\mu^2} = \frac{L^3 g \beta \Delta t}{\upsilon^2}$$

$$= \frac{(1.5)^3 \times 9.81 \times 0.003 \times (100 - 20)}{\left(18.97 \times 10^{-6}\right)^2} = 2.208 \times 10^{10}$$

$$Pr = \frac{\mu C_p}{k} = \frac{2 \times 10^{-5} \times 1004}{0.0289} = 0.6948$$

$$Gr \cdot Pr = 2.208 \times 10^{10} \times 0.6948 = 1.54 \times 10^{10}$$

$$Nu = \frac{hL_c}{k} = 0.10 \left(Gr\, Pr\right)^{1/3}$$

$$= 0.10 \left(1.54 \times 10^{10}\right)^{1/3} = 248.79$$

$$\therefore \quad h = \frac{248.79}{L} \times k$$

$$h = \frac{248.79 \times 0.0289}{1.5} = 4.793 \frac{W}{m^2\,{}^\circ C}$$

(Here Area is surface area of cylinder $= \pi DL$)

$\therefore$ Rate of heat loss, $Q = h \times$ Surface Area $\times \left(t_s - t_\infty\right),$

$$= 4.793 \times \left(\pi \times 0.18 \times 1.5\right)(100 - 20)$$

$$= \mathbf{325.27\ W}$$

OR

Q.3 A) 'It is desirable to use two thin fins instead of one thick fin for engine cooling'. Give reason.

Using two thin fins instead of one thick fin in engine cooling is desirable because thin fins have a higher surface area-to-volume ratio. This increases the effective surface area exposed to the cooling air, enhancing heat dissipation through convection.

Thick fins tend to have a temperature gradient inside the fin, causing the base to be much hotter than the tip, which reduces the overall heat transfer efficiency. Thin fins maintain a more uniform temperature throughout, improving heat transfer.

Additionally, two thin fins can create better airflow between them, increasing the convective heat transfer coefficient and thus cooling the engine more effectively.

B **Write the general differential equation in Cartesian co-ordinates for 3-D unsteady heat conduction by considering an infinitesimal volume element. Deduce there from the conduction equations for the following cases;**
(i) Steady state 1-D flow with heat generation at uniform rate within material, (ii) Unsteady 1-D flow without heat generation.

$$\frac{\partial}{\partial x}\left(k_x\frac{\partial t}{\partial x}\right)+\frac{\partial}{\partial y}\left(k_y\frac{\partial t}{\partial y}\right)+\frac{\partial}{\partial z}\left(k_z\frac{\partial t}{\partial z}\right)+\dot{q}_g = \rho.c.\frac{\partial t}{\partial \tau} \qquad \text{...(14)}$$

or, using the **vector operator** ∇, we get

$$\nabla.(k\nabla t)+\dot{q}_g = \rho.c.\frac{\partial t}{\partial \tau} \qquad \text{...(15)}$$

This is known as the general heat conduction equation for 'non-homogeneous anisotropic material', 'Self heat generating' and 'unsteady three-dimensional heat flow.'

Case (iii) Steady state and one-dimensional heat transer :

$$\frac{\partial^2 t}{\partial x^2}+\frac{\dot{q}_g}{k}=0$$

Case (vi) Unsteady state, one-dimensional, without internal heat generation :

$$\frac{\partial^2 t}{\partial x^2}=\frac{1}{\alpha}\cdot\frac{\partial t}{\partial \tau}$$

C **Consider two large parallel plates, one at 1000K with emissivity 0.8 and other is at 300K having emissivity 0.6. A radiation shield is placed between them. The shield has emissivity as 0.1 on the side facing hot plate and 0.3 on the side facing cold plate. Calculate percentage reduction in radiation heat transfer as a result of radiation shield.**

Given data: $\in_1 = 0.8, T_1 = 1000K, \in_2 = 0.6, T_2 = 600K, \in_{3h} = 0.1, \in_{3c} = 0.3$
(a) The heat transfer between two parallel plates by radiation is given by,

$$q = \frac{\sigma\left(T_1^4 - T_3^4\right)}{\dfrac{1}{\in_1}+\dfrac{1}{\in_3}-1} = \frac{5.67\left[\left(\dfrac{1000}{100}\right)^4-\left(\dfrac{300}{100}\right)^4\right]}{\dfrac{1}{0.8}+\dfrac{1}{0.6}-1} = \frac{5.67(10000-81)}{1.25+1.67-1}$$

$$= 29338W/m^2 = 29.34kW/m^2$$

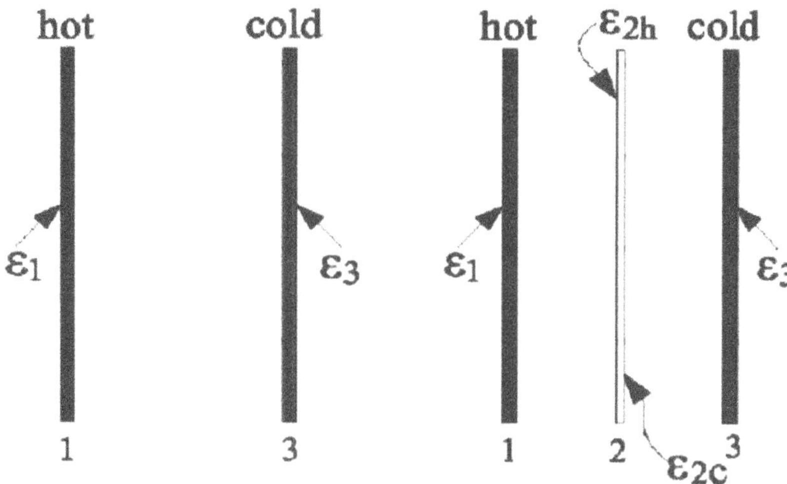

(b) When shield is kept between two plates, then for thermal equilibrium, we can write

$$q' = \frac{\sigma\left(T_1^4 - T_2^4\right)}{\dfrac{1}{\in_1} + \dfrac{1}{\in_{2h}} - 1} = \frac{\sigma\left(T_2^4 - T_3^4\right)}{\dfrac{1}{\in_{2c}} + \dfrac{1}{\in_3} - 1} \qquad ...(a)$$

Where T_2 is the temperature of the shield and $\in_{2h}$ and $\in_{2c}$ are the emissivities of the shield towards hot plate surface and cold plate surface.

Substituting the given values in equation (a)

$$\frac{\left[10^4 - \left(\dfrac{T_2}{100}\right)^4\right]}{\dfrac{1}{0.8} + \dfrac{1}{0.1} - 1} = \frac{\left[\left(\dfrac{T_2}{100}\right)^4 - (3)^4\right]}{\dfrac{1}{0.3} + \dfrac{1}{0.6} - 1}$$

$$\therefore \frac{10000 - x^4}{1.25 + 10 - 1} = \frac{x^4 - 81}{3.33 + 1.67 - 1}; \text{ where } x = \frac{T_2}{100}$$

$$\therefore \frac{10000 - x^4}{10.25} = \frac{x^4 - 81}{4}$$

$$\therefore 10000 - x^4 = 2.56 x^4 - 207.6$$

$$\therefore 3.56 x^4 = 10207.6$$

$$\therefore x^4 = 2867.3$$

$$\therefore x = \frac{T_2}{100} = 7.32$$

$$\therefore T_2 = 732K$$

The heat flow per m² area when shield is located is given by

$$q' = \frac{\sigma\left(T_1^4 - T_3^4\right)}{\dfrac{1}{\in_1} + \dfrac{1}{\in_{2h}} - 1}$$

$$= \frac{5.67\left[10^4 - 7.32^4\right]}{1.25 + 10 - 1} = \frac{5.67[7132.7]}{10.25} = 3946W \, / \, m^2 = 3.946kW \, / \, m^2$$

Percentage reduction in heat flow

$$= \frac{q - q'}{q} \times 100 = \frac{29.34 - 3.946}{29.34} \times 100 = 86.6\%$$

Q.4 **A) Give applications of heat exchangers.**

☐ Power Plants: Used to transfer heat from steam to water in boilers and condensers to generate electricity efficiently.

☐ Refrigeration and Air Conditioning: Employed to transfer heat from the refrigerant to the environment or vice versa, helping maintain desired temperatures.

☐ Chemical Processing: Used to control temperatures in reactors by heating or cooling process fluids.

☐ Automotive Industry: Radiators and oil coolers in vehicles use heat exchangers to maintain optimal engine and transmission temperatures.

☐ Food and Beverage Industry: Used for pasteurization and heating or cooling food products to ensure safety and quality.

☐ Waste Heat Recovery: Capture and reuse waste heat from industrial processes to improve overall energy efficiency.

B **What is insulation? State its four applications in engineering field.**

Insulation is a material or method used to reduce the rate of heat transfer between objects or environments at different temperatures.

☐ Thermal Insulation in Buildings: To reduce heat loss in winter and heat gain in summer, improving energy efficiency and comfort.

☐ Pipe Insulation: To prevent heat loss in hot fluid-carrying pipes or to protect cold pipes from freezing.

☐ Refrigeration Systems: To maintain low temperatures inside refrigerators and cold storage by minimizing heat ingress.

☐ Industrial Furnaces and Boilers: To retain heat within the system, improving fuel efficiency and protecting surrounding equipment.

C **What is condensation? Explain film-wise condensation and drop-wise condensation.**

Condensation is the physical process where a substance changes from its gaseous state to its liquid state. This occurs when the temperature of the vapor falls below its dew point or when the vapor comes into contact with a cooler surface. During condensation, the vapor molecules lose energy and come closer together, forming liquid droplets. This process is common in natural phenomena like dew formation, fog, and the water cycle, as well as in industrial applications such as heat exchangers and refrigeration systems.

Film-wise Condensation

Film-wise condensation occurs when the condensed liquid forms a continuous film or layer on the surface where condensation takes place. In this type, the condensate spreads over the surface, creating a thin liquid film that flows down due to gravity. The thermal resistance offered by this liquid film tends to reduce the heat transfer efficiency because the film acts as an insulating layer between the vapor and the cooler surface. Film-wise condensation is usually observed on clean and smooth surfaces where the liquid easily wets the surface.

Drop-wise Condensation

Drop-wise condensation happens when the condensed liquid forms discrete droplets on the surface rather than a continuous film. These droplets remain separated and do not spread out immediately. Because the droplets cover less surface area and allow direct contact between the vapor and the cooling surface, drop-wise condensation leads to higher heat transfer rates compared to film-wise condensation. This type of condensation is commonly seen on surfaces that are non-wetting or treated with hydrophobic coatings, which prevent the liquid from spreading.

OR

**Q.4
A)** **It is desirable to wear white clothes instead of black during the summer season. Give reason.**

Wearing white clothes during the summer is desirable because white reflects most of the sunlight and heat that falls on it, whereas black absorbs a large portion of the sunlight and heat. White clothing reflects radiant energy, keeping the body cooler by preventing excessive heat absorption. In contrast, black clothes absorb more heat, making the wearer feel warmer. Therefore, white clothes help in maintaining a cooler body temperature during hot weather, making them more comfortable to wear in the summer season.

B **Give eight examples related to heat transfer from the routine life.**

☐ Boiling Water on a Stove: Heat transfers from the burner to the pot by conduction, then to the water by convection.

☐ Feeling Warm Near a Fireplace: Heat is transferred by radiation from the fire to your body.

☐ Cooling of Hot Coffee: Heat is lost from the coffee to the surrounding air by convection and radiation.

☐ Touching a Metal Spoon in Hot Soup: Heat transfers from the soup to the spoon by conduction, making the spoon hot.

☐ Sweating on a Hot Day: Heat is removed from the body through evaporation, a cooling process.

☐ Sunlight Warming the Earth: Heat is transferred by radiation from the sun to the earth.

☐ Ice Melting in a Drink: Heat transfers from the warmer liquid to the ice by conduction, causing the ice to melt.

☐ Using a Thermos Flask: It reduces heat transfer by conduction, convection, and radiation to keep liquids hot or cold.

C **Derive the equation of LMTD for counter-flow heat exchangers.**

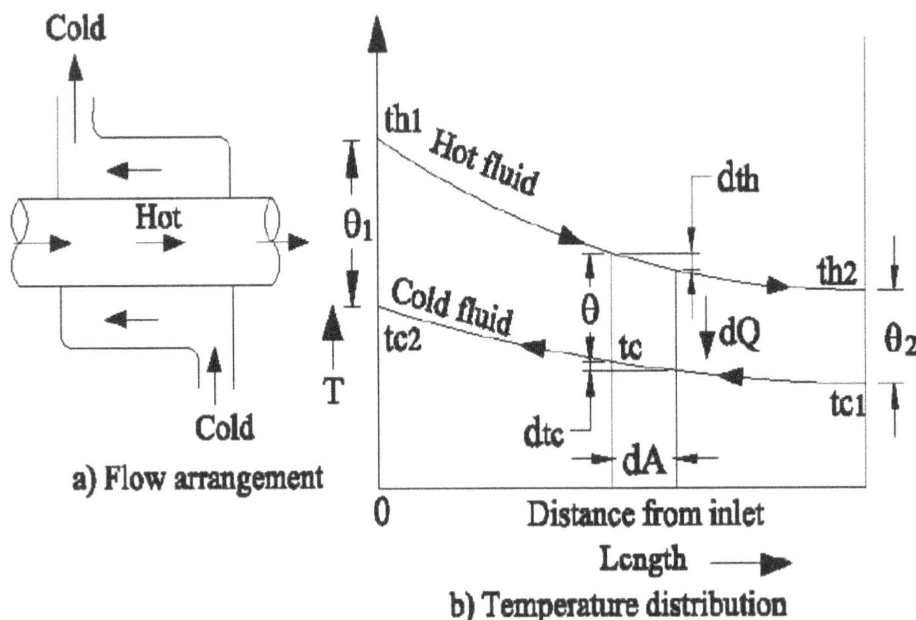

Figure 13 : Counter flow heat exchanger

Let us consider an elementary area dA of the heat exchanger. The rate of flow of heat through this elementary area is given by (Refer figure no. 13)

$$dQ = U \cdot dA\left(t_h - t_c\right) = U \cdot dA \cdot \Delta t$$

In this case also, the heat balance over a differential area dA may be written as

$$dQ = -\dot{m}_c \cdot c_{pc} \cdot dt_c = -\dot{m}_h \cdot c_{ph} \cdot dt_h$$

In a counter-flow system, the temperatures of both the fluids decrease in the direction of heat exchanger length, hence the negative signs.

$$\therefore dt_h = -\frac{dQ}{\dot{m}_h c_{ph}} = -\frac{dQ}{C_h}$$

$$\text{and,} \quad dt_c = -\frac{dQ}{\dot{m}_h c_{pc}} = -\frac{dQ}{C_c}$$

$$\therefore dt_h - dt_c = -dQ\left[\frac{1}{C_h} - \frac{1}{C_c}\right]$$

and
$$d\theta = -dQ\left[\frac{1}{C_h} - \frac{1}{C_c}\right]$$
...(11)

Inserting the value of dQ, we get

$$d\theta = -U\,dA\left(t_h - t_c\right)\left[\frac{1}{C_h} - \frac{1}{C_c}\right]$$

$$\therefore d\theta = -U\,dA\cdot\theta\left[\frac{1}{C_h} - \frac{1}{C_c}\right]$$

So,
$$\frac{d\theta}{\theta} = -U\,dA\cdot\left[\frac{1}{C_h} - \frac{1}{C_c}\right]$$

Integrating the above equation from $A = 0$ to $A = A$, we get

$$\ln\left(\theta_2 / \theta_1\right) = -U.A\left[\frac{1}{C_h} - \frac{1}{C_c}\right]$$

Now, the total heat transfer rate between the two fluids is given by

$$Q = C_h\left(t_{h1} - t_{h2}\right) = C_c\left(t_{c2} - t_{c1}\right)$$

So,
$$\frac{1}{C_h} = \frac{t_{h1} - t_{h2}}{Q}$$

and
$$\frac{1}{C_c} = \frac{t_{c2} - t_{c1}}{Q}$$

substituting the values of $\dfrac{1}{C_h}$ and $\dfrac{1}{C_c}$ in equation (12), we have,

$$\ln\left(\theta_2 / \theta_1\right) = -U\,A\left[\frac{t_{h1} - t_{h2}}{Q} - \frac{t_{c2} - t_{c1}}{Q}\right]$$

$$= -\frac{UA}{Q}\left[\left(t_{h1} - t_{c2}\right) - \left(t_{h2} - t_{c1}\right)\right] = -\frac{UA}{Q}\left(\theta_1 - \theta_2\right) = \frac{UA}{Q}\left(\theta_2 - \right.$$

or
$$Q = \frac{UA\left(\theta_2 - \theta_1\right)}{\ln\left(\theta_2 / \theta_1\right)}$$

Since,
$$Q = U\,A\,\theta_m$$

Q.5 **A) 'Radiator of automobiles is always painted black'. Give reason.**
The radiator of automobiles is always painted black because black surfaces are excellent emitters and absorbers of heat. Painting the radiator black helps it radiate heat more effectively from the hot coolant inside to the surrounding air.

This improves the cooling efficiency of the radiator by enhancing heat transfer through radiation, helping to keep the engine at an optimal temperature.

B   Define shape factor. Discuss salient features of shape factor.

The shape factor (also called view factor or configuration factor) between two surfaces is the fraction of the radiation leaving one surface that directly reaches and is intercepted by the other surface. It is denoted by F1→2.

It depends only on geometry, not on material properties or temperatures.

Salient Features of Shape Factor

6. Reciprocity Rule:

    A1F1→2=A2F2→1

    This relates the view factors between two surfaces.

7. Self-View Factor:

    o   For flat or convex surfaces, Fi→i=0 (they do not see themselves).

    o   For concave surfaces, Fi→i≠0.

8. Depends on Geometry:

    o   Shape factors are purely geometric and are independent of temperature or surface properties.

9. Used in Radiation Heat Transfer:

    o   Essential in calculating radiative exchange between surfaces in enclosures.

10. Symmetry in Shape Factor:

    o   Often used to simplify calculations in symmetrical geometries like parallel plates, concentric cylinders, or spheres.

C   An egg with mean diameter of 4 cm and initially at 20^0C is placed in a boiling water pan for 4 minutes and found to be boiled to the consumer's test.

For how long should a similar egg for same consumer be boiled when taken from a refrigerator at 5^0C.

Take following properties for egg :

k =10W/m^{0}C, ρ=1200kg /m^3, C =2kJ/kg^{0}C, h =100W/m$^{2\,0}$C

Given   data   : $R = \dfrac{40}{2} = 20mm = 0.02m, \quad t_i = 20°C, \quad \tau = 60 \times 4 = 240\sec,$

$k = 10W/m°C, \quad \rho = 1200kg/m^3, \quad c = 2000J/kg°C, \quad h = 100W/m^2 \cdot C$

For using the lump theory, the ref. condition is $Bi < 0.1$

$$Bi = \frac{h \cdot L_c}{k}$$

where, $L_c = \dfrac{v}{A_s} = \dfrac{\frac{4}{3}\pi R^3}{4\pi R^2} = \dfrac{R}{3}$

$$Bi = \frac{100 \times 0.02}{10 \times 3} = 0.067 < 0.1$$

we can use hemp theory.

a)   The temperature variation with time is given by

$$\frac{t-t_a}{t_i-t_a}=e^{-\frac{hA_\rho}{\rho vc}\tau}$$

$$\frac{h\cdot As}{\rho vc}=\left(\frac{h}{\rho C}\right)\left(\frac{As}{V}\right)=\left(\frac{100}{1200\times2000}\right)\left(\frac{3}{0.02}\right)=0.00625$$

$$\therefore\frac{t-100}{20-100}=e^{-0.0025\times240}=0.223$$

$$\therefore t=100+(20-100)\times0.223=82.16°C \qquad ...(a)$$

b)   Now, let us find 'τ' when the given data is :

$$t_i=5°C\ ,\ t_a=100°C\ \&\ t=82°C$$

$$\therefore\frac{82-100}{5-100}=e^{-0.00625\tau}=\frac{1}{e^{0.00625\tau}}$$

$$\therefore 0.1895=\frac{1}{e^{0.00625\tau}}$$

$$\therefore e^{0.00625\tau}=\frac{1}{0.1895}=5.277$$

$$\therefore 0.00625\tau=\ln5.277=1.6633$$

$$\therefore\tau=\frac{1.6633}{0.00625}=266.13\,\text{sec}$$

$$\tau=\textbf{4.435min} \qquad ...(b)$$

OR

Q.5 **During the summer season, vegetable vendors are sprinkling water to keep the**
A) **vegetable fresh. Evaluate in light of heat transfer.**

During the summer season, vegetable vendors sprinkle water on vegetables to keep them fresh. This practice can be explained through the principles of heat transfer, particularly evaporative cooling.

When water is sprinkled on the vegetables, it begins to evaporate due to the high ambient temperature. Evaporation is a cooling process, as it requires heat energy. This heat is absorbed from the surface of the vegetables and the surrounding air. As a result, the temperature of the vegetable surface drops, keeping them cool and fresh for a longer time.

By lowering the surface temperature, the vegetables lose moisture more slowly, which helps in reducing dehydration and wilting, thereby maintaining their appearance and quality even in hot weather.

Thus, the process utilizes latent heat of vaporization to transfer heat away from the vegetables, effectively slowing down spoilage through natural cooling.

B **Draw temperature variation for condenser and evaporator of thermal power plant.**

         Condenser   Evaporator

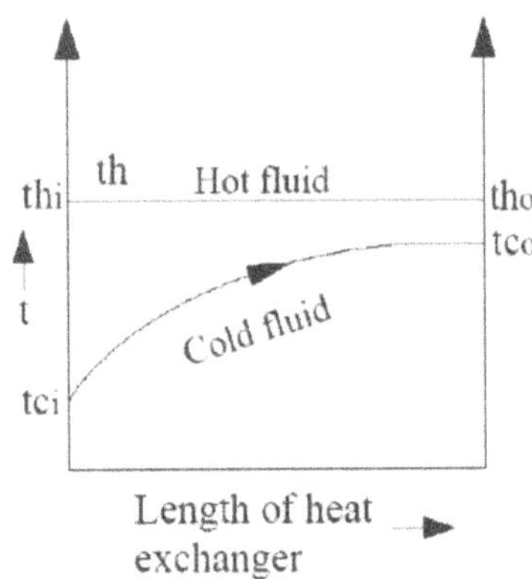

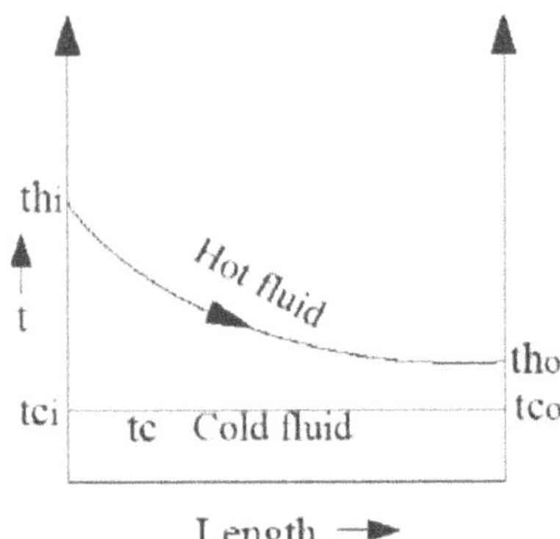

C   **Using dimensional analysis, obtain a general form of equation for forced convective heat transfer.**

Quantity	Symbol	Dimension
Heat Transfer co-efficient	h	$MT^{-3}\theta^{-1}$
Fluid Density	ρ	ML^{-3}
Length	l	L
Fluid Velocity	V	LT^{-1}
Fluid Viscosity	μ	$ML^{-1}T^{-1}$
Specific heat	C_p	$L^2T^{-2}\theta^{-1}$
Thermal conductivity	k	$MLT^{-3}\theta^{-1}$

→ Buckingham's π-theorem :

Total no. of quantities, $n = 7$ and Total no. of fundamental quantities, $m = 4$

∴ No. of π-constants $= n - m = 7 - 4 = 3$.

For obtaining π-groups, we would select length l (geometric), velocity V (flow characteristic), density ρ (fluid property) and thermal conductivity k (thermal property) as repeating variables.

π_1 - **terms :** $\pi_1 = l^{a_1}\, V^{b_1}\, \rho^{c_1}\, k^{d_1}\, h$

$$M^{o}L^{o}T^{o}\theta^{o} = [L]^{a_1} \left[LT^{-1}\right]^{b_1} \left[ML^{-3}\right]^{c_1} \left[MLT^{-3}\theta^{-1}\right]^{d_1} \left[MT^{-3}\theta^{-1}\right]$$

Equating exponents of M, L, T, θ we get

$$
\begin{aligned}
\text{For } M \;:\; & 0 = c_1 + d_1 + 1 \\
L \;:\; & 0 = a_1 + b_1 - 3c_1 + d_1 \\
T \;:\; & 0 = -b_1 - 3d_1 - 3 \\
\theta \;:\; & 0 = -d_1 - 1
\end{aligned}
$$

Equating above equations we get

$$a_1 = 1, \; b_1 = 0, \; c_1 = 0, \; d_1 = -1$$

Thus, $\pi_1 = l^1 V^0 \rho^0 k^{-1} h = \dfrac{hl}{k}$

π_2 -**term :** $\pi_2 = l^{a_2} V^{b_2} \rho^{c_2} k^{d_2} \mu$

Putting dimensions,

$$M^{o}L^{o}T^{o}\theta^{o} = [L]^{a_2} \left[LT^{-1}\right]^{b_2} \left[ML^{-3}\right]^{c_2} \left[MLT^{-3}\theta^{-1}\right]^{d_2} \left[ML^{-1}T^{-1}\right]$$

Equating exponents :

For M :   0 $= c_3 + d_3$
     L :   0 $= a_3 + b_3 - 3c_3 + d_3 + 2$
     T :   0 $= -b_3 - 3d_3 - 2$
     θ :   0 $= -d_3 - 1$

Equating above equations we get,

$$a_3 = 1, \ b_3 = 1, \ c_3 = 1, \ d_3 = -1$$

Thus, $\pi_3 = l^1 v^1 \rho^1 k^{-1} C_p = \dfrac{\rho v l}{k} \times C_p$

Now, this not popular dimensionless group. (or Prandtl No.)

Equating the dimensions of $\rho v l$ we get

$$\left[ML^{-3} \right]\left[LT^{-1} \right][L] = ML^{-1}T^{-1}$$

which is the dimension of viscosity μ, so we can use μ in place of $\rho v l$.

$$\therefore \pi_3 = \frac{\mu C_p}{k} \quad \text{(or Prandtl No.)}$$

Now considering $\phi\left(\pi_1 , \pi_2 , \pi_3 \right) = 0$ or $\phi\left(\dfrac{hl}{k} , \dfrac{\mu}{\rho v l} , \dfrac{\mu C_p}{k} \right) = 0$

or $\dfrac{hl}{k} = \phi\left(\dfrac{\mu}{\rho v l} , \dfrac{\mu C_p}{k} \right)$

or $\dfrac{hl}{k} = \phi\left(\dfrac{\rho v l}{\mu} , \dfrac{\mu C_p}{k} \right)$

or $Nu = \phi\left(Re, Pr \right)$

VIDEO LECTURE LINKS

1	Syllabus of Heat Transfer	https://youtu.be/xxuvvHux_Ww
2	Modes of Heat Transfer	https://youtu.be/Hh8xKBEUUOc
3	Thermal Conductivity and Cartesian Coordinate System	https://youtu.be/SZQSDKFzGf4
4	One Dimensional Heat Transfer, Electrical Analogy, heat transfer in Composite wall	https://youtu.be/qe1MJ4lJAzQ
5	Numerical for Conduction Heat transfer Cartesian Coordinate System	https://youtu.be/USMxGMoB9HU
6	Cylindrical Coordinate System with numerical _ Hollow cylinder and Composite Cylinder	https://youtu.be/eZGFPOtgUpY
7	Spherical Coordinate System with Numerical _ Hollow Sphere and Composite Sphere	https://youtu.be/Uy4Dhr3bfL4
8	Critical Radius of Insulation and Problems	https://youtu.be/iq8QqArd2WA
9	Rectangular Fin_ Extended Surfaces	https://youtu.be/LDo1kzECCtA
10	Heat Dissipation from Infinitely Long Fin	https://youtu.be/c72yWNv0ZXA
11	Heat Dissipation from a Fin Insulated at the Tip	https://youtu.be/Jc3pnIMS2E8
12	Fin with Finite Length and Heat Loss from the Tip by Convection	https://youtu.be/QYydig9Pz1E
13	Fin Effectiveness and Fin Efficiency	https://youtu.be/moDro0hsxtc
14	Estimation of Error in Temperature measurement with Thermometer Well	https://youtu.be/W9MQ9Ph3eUo
15	Unsteady State Heat Transfer	https://youtu.be/iKZalGBn4lo
16	Unsteady State Heat Transfer with Numerical_2	https://youtu.be/Snt8PYxU5zs

17	Fundamental of Heat Exchanger	https://youtu.be/_MJ83-_Xg6Y
18	Fundamental of Boiling and Condensation	https://youtu.be/X-Y7ZGK5IXQ
19	Heat transfer by Radiation _ Introduction	https://youtu.be/rs00ya0J6Is
20	Heat transfer by Radiation _ Governing Laws	https://youtu.be/dP7JfCg-_Ok
21	Numerical Related to Governing Laws of Heat transfer by radiation	https://youtu.be/yCXZ7pivus4
22	Shape factor and Numerical related to it	https://youtu.be/qeIWeOs89sA
23	Radiation Heat Exchange Between Non-Black Bodies	https://youtu.be/_iOyoEPMszQ
24	Electrical Network Analogy	https://youtu.be/5rgidhmFing
25	Radiation Shield with Numerical	https://youtu.be/b1uqVHoUXEg
26	Combined Radiation and Convection Heat Transfer with Numerical	https://youtu.be/VdswlKu1Gzw

YOUTUBE CHANNEL NAME: AVM TECH ANDROID

CHAPTER WISE IMPORTANT QUESTIONS

HEAT TRANSFER BY CONDUCTION

1. Define: 1) Critical thickness of insulation for cylinder 2) Thermal diffusivity 3) Thermal resistance

2. Define overall heat transfer co-efficient and write its equation for the spherical shell covered with a layer of insulation having heat transfer co-efficient at inner surface is hi and at outer surface is ho.

3. How is the thermal performance of a fin measured? Explain fin efficiency and effectiveness.

4. What are three modes of heat transfer? Explain their differences briefly with example.

5. Write a short note of critical radius of insulation.

6. Differentiate fin efficiency and fin effectiveness.

7. "Generally, fin is provided to increase the heat transfer rate but by providing fin heat transfer may decrease" Justify the statement analytically.

8. Differentiate between steady and unsteady state heat transfer.

9. Differentiate between heat transfer and mass transfer.

10. Differentiate between conduction and radiation.

11. Write the general differential equation in Cartesian co-ordinates for 3-D unsteady heat conduction by considering an infinitesimal volume element.
Deduce there from the conduction equations for the following cases; (i) Steady state 1-D flow with heat generation at uniform rate within material. (ii) Unsteady 2-D flow without heat generation.

12. Explain aims to study 'Heat Transfer'.

13. 'Aluminum utensils are not desirable to use for cooking purposes. Evaluate.

14. State and explain Fourier's law for heat transfer. Mention the assumptions on which it is based. Define thermal conductivity and give its unit.

15. Derive the expression for the temperature distribution and heat dissipation from a fin insulated at the tip.

16. What is Critical thickness? Why an insulated small diameter wire has a higher current carrying capacity than an uninsulated one?

17. Write the most general equation in Cartesian co-ordinates for heat transfer by conduction.
Deduce above equation for the following cases;
      a) Steady state, one dimensional heat transfer with internal heat generation,
      b) Two dimensional heat transfer without heat generation, and
      c) Steady state, one dimensional heat transfer without internal heat generation.

18. Write the differential equation for steady state heat conduction in cylinder without heat generation. Reduce that equation for radial heat conduction and solve the equation.

19. Define Biot number. What is the physical significance of it? The Biot number during a heat transfer process between sphere and it surrounding is 0.02. Would you use lumped system analysis for determining the centre temperature of the sphere? Why?

20. What is meant by thermal resistance? Explain the electrical analogy for solving heat transfer problems.
21. What is the significance of 'Heat Transfer' in your branch? Explain in details with suitable examples.
22. Write a short note of critical radius of insulation.
23. Explain how fins can increase the rate of heat transfer. Mention the most common types of fins and sketch them. Give some practical examples of fins.

HEAT TRANSFER BY CONVECTION

24. Define thermal boundary layer and hydrodynamic boundary layer. Draw them for very low Prandtl number fluid.
25. Write the value of critical Reynolds Number for flow over a flat plate. Differentiate viscous sub layer and buffer layer.
26. Define: 1) Nusselt number 2) Grashoff Number 3) Peclet number
27. Define: hydrodynamic and thermal boundary layer. Represent their respective thickness for high Prandtl number fluid
28. Explain and differentiate natural and forced convection.
29. Explain geometric similarity, kinematic similarity and dynamic similarity with example.
30. Explain Displacement thickness, Momentum thickness and Energy thickness.
31. Differentiate between free convection and forced convection.
32. Differentiate between Nusselt number and Reynolds number.
33. 'It is desirable to use two thin fins instead of one thick fin for engine cooling'. Justify.
34. Using Buckingham – π theorem show that Nusselt number for free convection is a function of Grashoff Number and Prandtl number.
35. Using Buckingham – π theorem show that Nu = f (Re, Pr) for forced convection.
36. What is the limitation of Rayleigh's method of dimensional analysis? Which method is preferred in such case and how repeating variables are selected?
37. Differentiate between Nusselt number and Biot number.
38. Using dimensional analysis, obtain a general form of equation for Natural Convective heat transfer.
39. Explain the concept of hydrodynamic and thermal boundary layers. Superimpose hydrodynamic and thermal boundary layer profiles for Pr < 1, Pr = 1 and Pr > 1
40. Derive Von-Karman integral momentum equation for hydrodynamic boundary layer over a flat plate. Solve this equation for cubical velocity profile and derive the expression for hydrodynamic boundary layer thickness.

HEAT TRANSFER BY RADIATION

41. State Wien's displacement law and write its significance.
42. Define gray body. Differentiate between surface resistance and space resistance w.r.to radiation heat transfer between two grey bodies.
43. Define: 1) Radiosity 2) Absorptivity 3) Total emissive power
44. Define and differentiate black body and grey body.
45. Write four properties of shape factor.

46. What do you understand by absorptivity? How can it be improved for an opaque body?
47. Define radiation heat transfer coefficient? On what factor does it depend?
48. Differentiate between counter-flow and parallel flow heat exchanger.
49. 'In summer, one should wear white clothes instead of black one.' Why?
50. Define radiation shield. Prove that if radiation shield of the emissivity same as the emissivity of two parallel plate is inserted between two parallel plates net heat transfer rate due to radiation is reduced to half as compared to without shield.
51. Derive the expression for net radiant heat exchange between two infinites parallel planes.
52. 'Radiator of automobiles is always painted black'. Give reason.
53. Explain Kirchhoff's law in detail.
54. What is Plank's law? Explain it in detail and discuss that it is basic law of thermal radiation?
55. What is Stefan-Boltzmann law? How is it derived from Plank's law of thermal radiation?

HEAT EXCHANGER

56. Define fouling of heat exchanger. Write equation of fouling factor and enlist parameter affecting fouling.
57. Define heat exchanger and state differences between recuperative and regenerative type of heat exchanger.
58. Draw the sketch of variation of temperature along the length for parallel and counter flow heat exchangers and write their comparisons.
59. What is a compact heat exchanger? Write their key areas of applications.
60. What do you understand by fouling factor in case of heat exchanger? List the causes of fouling.
61. What do you understand by TEMA charts? How are they useful in the design of multi-pass heat exchangers?
62. Draw temperature variation for condenser of power plant.
63. How heat exchangers are classified?
64. What do you understand by NTU method in case of heat transfer? Derive its expression following the usual notations for parallel flow heat exchanger.
65. Derive the equation of LMTD for counter-flow heat exchangers.
66. Derive the equation of effectiveness-NTU method for the parallel- flow heat exchangers.
67. Derive the relationship between the effectiveness and the number of transfer units for a counter flow heat exchanger.

BOILING AND CONDENSATION

68. Define Boiling. Draw the boiling curve for water and show different regimes on that. Explain Nucleate boiling regime and factors affecting it.
69. State the regimes of pool boiling and define process of condensation.
70. Explain dropwise condensation and film condensation.